To Simon,

Keep it
Real!

TEEN DADS

Other Books by Jeanne Warren Lindsay:

Teens Parenting—Your Baby's First Year

Teens Parenting—The Challenge of Toddlers

You Can Help Pregnant and Parenting Teens:
Curriculum Guide for Teens Parenting Series

Do I Have a Daddy? A Story About a Single-Parent Child

School-Age Parents: Challenge of Three-Generation Living

Teenage Marriage: Coping with Reality

Teens Look at Marriage: Rainbows, Roles and Reality

Parents, Pregnant Teens and the Adoption Option

Pregnant Too Soon: Adoption Is an Option

Open Adoption: A Caring Option

By Jeanne Lindsay and Jeanne Brunelli

Teens Parenting—Your Pregnancy and Newborn Journey

Adolescentes como padres—La jornada de tu embarazo
y el nacimiento de tu bebé

By Jeanne Lindsay and Sally McCullough
Teens Parenting—Discipline from Birth to Three

By Jeanne Lindsay and Sharon Rodine:

Teen Pregnancy Challenge, Book One:
Strategies for Change

Teen Pregnancy Challenge, Book Two:
Programs for Kids

By Jeanne Lindsay and Catherine Monserrat:

Adoption Awareness: Help for Teachers,
Counselors, Nurses and Caring Others

TEEN DADS

Rights, Responsibilities and Joys

Jeanne Warren Lindsay, MA, CHE

Photographs by David Crawford, MA

Morning Glory Press

Buena Park, California

Library of Congress Cataloging-in-Publication Data

Lindsay, Jeanne Warren.
    Teen dads : rights, responsibilities and joys / Jeanne Warren
Lindsay.
        p.   cm.
    Includes bibliographical references and index.
    Summary: A guide for teenage fathers who want to develop their
parenting skills, with an emphasis on dealing with children from

                            95. -- ISBN 0-930934-78-4 (pbk.) :

    1. Teenage fathers--Juvenile literature. 2. Child rearing--
Juvenile literature. 3. Parenting--Juvenile literature.
[1. Teenage fathers.   2. Child rearing.   3. Parenting.]   I. Title.
HQ756.7.L56   1993   93-4450
649.1'0243--dc20   CIP
                                                          AC

MORNING GLORY PRESS, INC.
6595 San Haroldo Way   Buena Park, CA 90620-3748
(714) 828-1998
Printed and bound in the United States of America

Contents

Acknowledgments

I'm most grateful to the 41 young fathers I interviewed especially
for this book. Some of these young men gave me permission to thank
them by name. They include Matthew Topchi, Jose Sanchez, Mizraim
Leal, Chris Rismiller, Albert Aguilar, Ryan Hollmann, Jason Kucharek,
Harry Lyles, Ruben Nora, Richard L. Ellison, Edgar Alcala, Frank
Villalobos, Herman Hernandez, Chris Mitchell, Dana Broshar, John
Bernardino, Sam Thompson, Gary Gracely, Jr., Jason Brinckman,
Eddie Escobar, Carl Miller, Jason Taylor, Sam Vasquez, Rob Black-
mon, Chris Focht, An Njuyen, and Ray Ramirez.

Rita Vogel, GRADS teacher at Buckeye Youth Center, Ohio
Department of Youth Services, Columbus, Ohio, assisted by Nancy
Nicolisi, made arrangements for me to interview nine teenage fathers at
the Buckeye Youth Center, and Lisa Montoya arranged for me to visit
and interview four teen fathers incarcerated in Ventura, California. I
appreciate the candidness of these young men in sharing with me their
feelings concerning their children and their children's mothers.

Others who referred clients for interviewing and/or provided other
help include Lynn Coleman, Julie Vetica, Pat Alviso, David Crawford,
Kenneth Easum, Annette Cooper, Peggy McNabb, Barbara Kolar, Pat
Clark, Teresa Branham, Steve Burkhard, and Paula Cross.

Nagel Vann, Program Officer of the Public/Private Ventures Young
Unwed Fathers Pilot Project, wrote the informative and positive
Foreword. I appreciate his help, and most of all, I appreciate all he's
doing for young fathers through this program.

David Crawford, in addition to providing the photos of teen fathers
and their children, edited the manuscript and provided encouragement
and guidance. I treasure his help and friendship. For more about David,
see page 184.

Others who reviewed the manuscript and made many helpful
suggestions include Edwin Woodley, Rita Vogel, Julie Vetica, Jean
Brunelli, PHN, co-author of *Teens Parenting—Your Pregnancy and
Newborn Journey;* Sally McCullough, co-author of *Teens Parenting—
Discipline from Birth to Three;* Matthew Topchi, teen father who sug-
gested I write a book for teen dads; and a young father at Buckeye
Youth Center who read the manuscript and made many helpful notes.

Tim Rinker designed the cover using a photo from David. Erin
Lindsay, Carole Blum, and Karen Blake proofread the manuscript. I
appreciate and love them.

Most of all, I appreciate Bob, the wonderful father of our children
and my love for 42 years.

Jeanne Lindsay

Preface

Teenage fathers as a group have a poor reputation. The baby's mother's parents may think the pregnancy was his fault. They don't want him to see their daughter again. At the same time, they may expect the young father to support his child.

If he's 16, he may indeed be irresponsible. Acting irresponsibly is typical behavior for many 16-year-olds. He may not be able to get a job, and if he does, he won't make enough money to support his family.

He may be in a real bind. His child's maternal grandparents, and perhaps his child's mother, don't want him around. It's impossible for him to fulfill his responsibilities adequately. No wonder many teen fathers bow out of the parenting scene.

Even if he stays around, he may not know much about

the art and skills of parenting. If he's awkward as he tries to diaper his baby, mom may laugh at him. If he doesn't live with mom, is she willing for him to visit regularly? If he sees his child only occasionally, how can he relate to his son or daughter?

This book is meant to help a young father learn to parent. Forty-one teenage fathers were interviewed especially for *Teen Dads,* and they are frequently quoted to reinforce the concepts presented. As each young father is quoted, he is identified by his age and the ages of his child(ren) and the child(ren)'s mother. If the same parent is quoted again in the same chapter, only his name is listed. Names have been changed, but the quotes and the ages given are always real.

Teen Dads covers the parenting basics. If you want more detailed guidance, see the *Teens Parenting* series of books. *Teens Parenting—Your Baby's First Year* and *Teens Parenting—The Challenge of Toddlers* are written directly to teenage parents. *Teens Parenting—Discipline from Birth to Three* is an especially good supplement to **Teen Dads.**

If you are a teenage father, you probably love your child dearly. You'd like to be the best possible parent. You also want to deal with such issues as your relationship with your child's mother and her family and planning for your future. **Teen Dads** is written especially to help you meet your goals in parenting—to be a good father and to live the most satisfying life possible.

Best wishes and good luck!

Jeanne Lindsay
May, 1993

Foreword

What does it mean to be a "teen dad"?

When asked that question, many people picture an irresponsible young man who has fathered multiple children with different mothers, then walked away from each without another thought. While some teen fathers may reinforce this stereotype, the reality is usually very different. Data from ethnographic and other studies indicate that most young fathers try to accept the responsibilities of fatherhood, though they often succeed only intermittently.

Teen parenthood is by no means a recent phenomenon. However, the circumstances surrounding it are vastly different than they were just a few years ago. And while the number of births to teenage mothers has declined over the past twenty years (from 656,000 in 1970 to 533,000 in 1990), the number of births to *unmarried* mothers has increased (from 200,000 to 361,000).

Not all of the fathers of these children are teens, but they are generally no older than 25. In 1990, 58 percent of teen mothers reported the age of the baby's father on the birth certificate; of these mothers, 32 percent indicated a teen father, and 52 percent reported the father's age as between 20 and 24.

Most are at a critical point in their lives. Already dealing with the myriad issues involved in moving from adolescence to adulthood, they are being asked also to consider how to provide for the significant needs of a young child.

While the number of unmarried teen births has increased, the range of jobs available to young men has changed. In 1970, a young man could drop out of high school, but still expect to find a job that paid a wage on which he could support a family. That is no longer the case. Between 1973 and 1992, the median real weekly earnings of full-time employed males aged 16 to 24 fell almost 30 percent. Comparable earnings of males 25 and over fell only 7 percent from 1973 to 1990.

The public policy response to these changes initially focused primarily on the teen mother. Numerous programs were established to provide them with prenatal care and parenting services. And as the number of single mothers increased—and consequently the number of AFDC recipients—many have been placed in job training programs.

More recently, attention has begun to focus on involving the "absent" or "noncustodial" father, but the emphasis has too often been on financial responsibility, i.e., the obligation to make regular child support payments.

While there is no doubt that all fathers should take such responsibility, the kind of approaches taken have not acknowledged the reduced income potential of young men or the desire of most young fathers to be good fathers to their children. Rather, what they lack is not the desire to take responsibility, but the support they need as they attempt to make a dual transition—from adolescence to adulthood, and from non-parent to parent.

As more and more people around the country have come to

share this conclusion, a good number of programs have been established in many states to provide support mechanisms for young fathers. However, most of these are understaffed and underfunded, and often struggle to provide the full array of services that are needed. There are also a few states that operate programs for noncustodial parents, but most of these are focused on job placements for older fathers rather than the more diverse needs of young fathers.

Public/Private Ventures' (P/PV) Young Unwed Fathers Pilot Project, which has been operating in six sites around the country since March, 1991, is attempting to shed more light on how best to support such fathers. Although the early project findings provide no definitive answers, they certainly do not support the stereotype of "deadbeat dads."

In fact, of the 228 fathers included in the early project research, 70 percent report that they see their children at least once a week; 63 percent report having only one child; only 18 percent had children by more than one mother. Large percentages reported bathing (46 percent), feeding (81 percent), dressing (73 percent), and playing with (87 percent) their child.

In designing the Young Unwed Fathers Pilot Project, which serves fathers aged 16 to 25, P/PV has sought to get a better picture of who these young men are; to determine which program models and services are most effective in attracting and serving them; and to demonstrate ways in which employment and training agencies, child support enforcement agencies, welfare departments, and community-based agencies can work together to increase the chances that young fathers will find and hold jobs that will enable them to support themselves and their children over the long term.

As of this writing, the "jury is still out" on these goals—the final report on the pilot project is not due until December, 1993. It has certainly not been an easy process for either staff or participants, and that is an important message for all young fathers or teen dads reading this book. We have, however, seen that it is possible for young men to stay involved with their children and, with the help of dedicated program staff, for them to begin working toward long-term educational and occupational goals.

In particular, the fathers at the P/PV sites have responded to participation in support groups, built around P/PV's Fatherhood Development curriculum, that enable them to share their experiences, form bonds with each other and program staff, and provide each other with ongoing support as they move through the program.

By reading *Teen Dads: Rights, Responsibilities and Joys,* teen fathers and program staff who work with them will have the opportunity to experience similar achievements. Readers will gain knowledge of what it means to be a father, learn how other young men have responded to the challenges of fatherhood, and begin to develop their own strategies for being a good father for their children now and as those children grow up.

Teen fathers will probably get the most benefit from this book if they are reading it with other fathers and discussing issues as they relate to each of their current experiences and situations, but those fathers who read it on their own will also have taken an important first step.

For all the teen dads who do pick this book up: I wish you good luck in the great adventure of fatherhood. Most important, good luck to your children. Help them to grow up feeling safe and secure so that they can be successful, enjoy life, and be good parents to your grandchildren.

Nigel Vann, Project Officer
Young Unwed Fathers Pilot Project
Public/Private Ventures
Philadelphia, Pennsylvania

To the young fathers
who share their wisdom
on these pages

*"A good dad is someone who takes time to be there,
to keep the family together. I'd like to be a good dad."* (Ray)

CHAPTER 1

Especially For Dad

A good dad is someone who takes time out of his life to be there, to keep the family together, to be with the mom and the baby, to play with them, just be a dad. I'd like to be a good dad.

Ray, 15 (Adonna, 16, six months pregnant)

Having a baby changed my life a lot. I had to stop doing about everything, going to parties, hanging out. I had to focus on Jaysay, meeting his needs.

I have to be mature and stand up for whatever he needs, be a man because I've got responsibilities now.

Darrance, 17 - Jaysay, 1 year (Victoria, 17)

If you're a teen father—or will be soon—what about you? People say teen fathers don't care about their babies. They only want to make girls pregnant. They say teenage

fathers forget about their children and their children's
mothers.

Some teen fathers don't get involved. Some seem not to
care about their children. But you probably aren't like that.
If you were, you wouldn't be reading this book.

Perhaps you live with your baby's mother. You may be
married, although only one in three teenage mothers is
married when her baby is born. See Chapter 13 for
suggestions regarding the marriage decision.

If You Don't Live with Your Baby

You may have a close relationship with your baby's
mother even if you're not living together. Perhaps you took
prepared childbirth classes together. You may have been
deeply involved coaching the mother throughout labor and
delivery. Perhaps you're caring for the baby as much as
you can.

If the baby's parents are not married, how much
"should" the father be included? If the young family lives
together, they probably feel much the same about joint
parenting as do married couples. If they don't live together,
there is no pattern cut and ready for them to follow.

Many fathers who don't live with their children want a
strong relationship with them. Kyle is an example:

*Last night when Dorene came over, I was going
out. All my friends were outside waiting for me, and
here comes the mom with the baby. So I told my
friends to go on—I was going to stay with my baby.*

*At first I was disappointed because I wanted to go
out with my friends. Then Liliane ran toward me
smiling, and I knew I wanted to stay with her. My
baby comes first, although sometimes it's really hard
for me.*

Kyle, 16 - Liliane, 15 months (Dorene, 16)

Miguel lived with his daughter's mother for several months after Genevieve was born. In fact, if he had his way, he would still be living with his family. Since that's impossible, he spends as much time with Genevieve as he can:

> *I'll continue to keep Genevieve whenever I can and buy her things she needs. If I go shopping, it's not me I have on my mind, it's them, and I'll buy them something.*
>
> *Today I didn't go to work so I kept Genny all day. She's not only my daughter—she's like a little friend. I was playing with her all day. She's all active—she gets me tired, but I love her so much I'd do anything for her. She goes in all the rooms, and I have to be alert. She's smart. She does things I wouldn't think she would do. I'll tell her to go get me a diaper. She'll do it, and I'll give her a hug. Every time she does something good, I hug her.*
>
> Miguel, 20 - Genevieve, 18 months (Maurine, 16)

If You and Mom Aren't Together

If you aren't with your baby's mother, you can still have a relationship with your child. Unless the court forbids it, you have a right to see your child and to spend time with him. If you aren't able to provide for him financially at this point, share your time.

> *First, I'm going to go up to her house all the time even if we're split up, and see if I can take the baby on weekends. I'll probably end up going through court trying to get legal rights to see him every weekend.*
>
> Devin, 16 (Tiffany, 17 - 9 months pregnant)

In some states, visitation is tied to providing child support, but this is not the case in most states. The father

usually has the right to see his child whether or not he's
paying support.

Legally, he may be able to have his child part of the
time. Some fathers have custody of their children. Parents
who don't agree should talk to a lawyer or legal aid group.

Establishing Paternity

If you and your baby's mother are not married, it's
important that you establish paternity. This means that you
both sign legal papers stating you are the father of your
child. If you don't, your child might not be able to claim
Social Security, insurance benefits, veterans' and other
types of benefits through you. This is also the only legal
way for an unmarried father to establish his right to visitation or custody. See Chapter 15 for more information on
this subject.

When you visit your child, keep a record of these visits.
Get written receipts for the money you provide for child
support. You'll need these written records if you go
to court.

Incidentally, try not to make verbal threats to baby's
mother. Making threats could be held against you in court
which might lead to you being denied visitation rights.
Besides, your baby will be ahead if you and his mother,
even if you aren't together, can put your differences aside
when you're talking about your child.

Your child needs you. If you aren't through school yet,
you may not be able to pay your share of his support.
Instead, this is the time to obtain job skills so that you'll be
able soon to pay for at least half of your child's needs.

You don't need to wait until you're older to give your
child your love, caring, and emotional support. Even if you
can't pay all the bills at this point, you can be supportive in
many other ways. That's what this book is all about.

It's Not Easy

Andy discussed the difficulties of having a child before he was ready. He speaks for many young fathers:

The hard thing is you're still a kid. You can't deny it. You got yourself into this mess.

I wish I had never had kids. There are a lot of things I'd like to be doing now, but I can't change what I've done. I have to deal with it even though sometimes I say, "This sucks." I see my friends who don't have kids, and I wish I were like them.

Now I have to think about my baby when I'm walking on the street. It feels weird. Before, I didn't have anyone to think about except me. Now I have to watch out for all three of us. I was mostly raised to take care of myself. I understood there wouldn't be anybody there to help me out.

Now I have to think of them. It's hard.

Andy, 17 - Gus, 5 months (Yolanda, 15)

Of course it's hard. Parenting a child is one of the hardest—and one of the most rewarding—tasks faced by human beings. Getting pregnant before she's ready changes a young woman's life. It also changes your life.

Many teen fathers choose to support and share in their child's care. They do so even though they may face hardship and broken dreams just as their baby's mother does. They know how important a father's influence is on his son or daughter.

When you choose this route, you will see your baby grow. First, you'll see her become a charming and independent toddler. You can be there as she travels through childhood. Finally, you can see her become a responsible, mature adult. *What a wonderful opportunity!*

"What would you do if we had a kid?" (Marc)

CHAPTER 2

Is She
Pregnant?

*When Melinda told me she was pregnant, I didn't
come home. I went out to a friend's house and got
plastered. I said, "Well, she's been asking me for
awhile, saying 'What would you do if we had a kid?'"*

*I was overwhelmed. I was living with my father,
and he kicked me out. He said, "You've got to take
responsibility, you've got to get a job and go take
care of her." So I went to live with her.*

Marc, 16 - Koary, 14 months (Melinda, 18)

*It was on Thanksgiving Day. She phoned me and
said she was pregnant. At first I thought, "Maybe she
just thinks she is. How could I get somebody pregnant?" Then I got to thinking. Was it mine or somebody else's? You know, all that.*

I used to go around doing whatever I wanted.
Finally I realized she was pregnant with my kid. Then
I started caring more and more. I felt there was a
little of me in that baby along with a little of her.
That's a good feeling.

My friends would say, "You're going to be a
father?" They was cool about it.

One buddy said, "Man, you ain't going to have no
money. Everything you make is going for this kid."

Everybody else wanted to be the godfather.

I'm supposed to graduate in four months. Then I
want to go in the Air Force. We'll get married after
she graduates in two years. I want to be involved with
my baby all the way. My kid will come first.

Norm, 17 (LaTisha, 15, 9 months pregnant)

Early Pregnancy Test Is Vital

Do you and your partner think she might be pregnant but
aren't sure? Please help her see a doctor. Getting an early
pregnancy test is important for several reasons:

- She might not be pregnant. If she isn't, and you and she
  don't want her to be pregnant, you have two choices:
  Don't have sex. If you do, use birth control.
- She has more choices early in her pregnancy. She
  could choose to have an abortion. An abortion is safer
  and easier for the woman if it's done during the first 12
  weeks of pregnancy. She has the legal right to decide
  for or against abortion whether or not you agree.
- She needs to see the doctor if she's continuing her
  pregnancy. The doctor will help her care for the unborn
  baby so it will be born healthy.
- Some couples choose to release the baby for adoption.
  Adoption planning is best done fairly early in the
  pregnancy although the final decision cannot be made
  until after the baby is born.

Important as prenatal care is, doctors cost a lot. Do you have health insurance through your work? Or can she get prenatal care through her family's health plan? If not, can she get MedicAid? Call your local Department of Public Social Services (Welfare Department) to find out.

Some areas have prenatal health clinics. Women can get prenatal check-ups for no charge, or they may be charged according to their income.

How Do *You* Feel About This Pregnancy?

Learning his partner is pregnant makes some teenage fathers happy. At the same time, they may feel scared as they think of the responsibilities they're facing.

Esteban and Trudy were both 15 when Trudy became pregnant. At first, Esteban tried not to think about it. At the same time, he didn't want to desert his child:

It was a shock to me. I didn't want to be a father. I was too young. I thought we was just playing around. Then all at once Trudy came up with something real serious. She lived around the block from me, and I tried to avoid her.

I ran away from it for awhile. Then I went back to Trudy. My dad left when I was born. I didn't want that for my baby.

Trudy was moody, always snapping. She was scared, too, but she didn't pressure me. I kept telling her I wasn't going to leave her.

I wasn't with her in the hospital. That was because her dad don't like me. I didn't see Nathan until he was a week old.

I used to hang out on the streets while Trudy was pregnant. After Nathan was born I changed. When I saw my kid, how he looked like me, I calmed down.

I quit school because we didn't have any money.

I got a job. Then I started back to school last fall.
Next month I'm going back on Independent Study. We
need more money, so I have to go back to work.
                    Esteban, 18 - Nathan, 2; Ralph, 5 months (Trudy, 17)

Your child needs your love and care. He also needs your
financial support. Both parents are required by law to
support their child.

I was scared when she told me she was pregnant.
I was working, but I didn't know how I was going to
support her and the baby. I couldn't even support
myself. I was also real excited. I was happy, but I
was scared.

I knew everything was going to be different.
Nothing would ever be the same again. I felt like my
freedom was going to be taken away. I couldn't come
and go as I pleased, but I wanted to do the right
thing. I wanted my daughter to have a father.
                          Carlos, 19 - Elena, 23 months (Monica, 18)

Her Parents May Reject You

I had problems with her mom, and we were always
hostile. I really didn't like her, and she didn't like me.
She had Aracely at 17, and she didn't want the same
thing for Aracely.
                          Sergio, 17 - Yvette, 11 months (Aracely, 17)

Your partner's parents may not want you around. Their
daughter is no longer a carefree teenager. She is now or
soon will be a hardworking mother, and they may
blame you.

Her parents and I were pretty close. When they
learned Darlene was pregnant, they had anger for
me. I wasn't wanted in their house. Now that the baby
is born, they're pretty happy. They like me again.

> *It really puts you down when they reject you.*
> *That's what they were doing. I stuck in there because*
> *in my heart I wanted to be with my child.*
> *I would say to Darlene, "I understand why they*
> *feel like that, but why don't they give us a chance?"*
> Manual, 18 - Juan, 27 months; Darcy, 13 months (Darlene, 18)

If you have this problem with your partner's parents, perhaps you can convince them you're their grandchild's father, and that you want to do your best to parent your child well. They may realize that you are, indeed, a positive influence on this grandchild they probably adore.

> *It will work. When her dad used to get mad at me*
> *and tell me to get out of this place, I'd leave. Then I'd*
> *come back the next day, and we would settle our*
> *problems.*
> *The more we talk and the more we get closer, the*
> *better it will be.*
> Alvaro, 17 (Sophia, 17 - 6 months pregnant)

"I was scared when she told me she was pregnant." (Carlos)

Don't Drop Out!

Some young men drop out of school when they learn
their partner is pregnant. They feel they must get a job and
support their family.

Is this how you feel? It's a hard decision. If you drop out
of school, you probably won't get a well-paying job.
Without even a high school diploma, you may never be
able to support your family as you'd like. If you must go
to work full-time, you should enroll in your school's
Independent or Work Study program.

Most young people need good career counseling. Perhaps your school can tell you about job training. Intensive
job training now can help you get a job with a future.

*For several years I ditched school. I didn't like the
teachers, and I got behind.*

*I went to the Marines to see how I could join. They
said I'm too young, and that I had to have a high
school diploma. That's when I went back to school. I
signed up for night school, too. I even do my
homework now.*

Sergio

Fathers and mothers who continue their education and
hold good jobs obviously are much better off than are parents who quit school and whose only income is their grant
from AFDC (Aid to Families with Dependent Children).

*First I want to get my GED (General Equivalency
Diploma) and start moving on, then train with com-
puters. I worry about the future a little. I don't want
to be real old and still making minimum wage. I want
to be financially secure.*

Miguel, 20 - Genevieve, 18 months (Maurine, 16)

Shaun was enrolled in college when he learned he'd be

a father soon. With help from his parents, he's staying in school. He says this is the best thing he can do now:

I was shocked at the pregnancy test. I cried with her. For a couple of weeks you can't think. I was in college and knew I wanted to stay there. I'd have a baby to take care of. I had to get through college. I hoped my parents would understand and help me, and they have.

If I didn't stay in school, I couldn't get a good job. I could work at some job with no future. I'd rather struggle the next couple of years. That's better than struggling for the rest of our lives.

Shaun, 19 - Troy, 2 months (Bethann, 17)

Importance of School for Mom

I was very upset that she quit going to school. I'd like her out of school as soon as possible. Her high school diploma is very important, and she agrees.

Shaun

Is your partner in school? If she hasn't graduated, it's important that she continue her education. She, like you, needs an education and job skills.

It's not legal for public schools to push students out of school because of pregnancy or because they're married. However, she might prefer a special program for school-age parents. Ask the school counselor if there is such a program in her school district. If she chooses a special program, she can take prenatal health and parenting classes. She can also get help in solving problems caused by her pregnancy.

If you're a student at the school, you should be able to enroll in the special class with her. In fact, if your school has a parenting class, you should be welcome whether or not your baby's mother is a student there.

Adoption Is Still an Option

Most pregnant teens either have an abortion or they
continue their pregnancy and parent their child themselves.
There is another option, however—adoption.

A generation or two ago, many unmarried pregnant teens
released their babies for adoption. They agreed to let
another family parent the child. The birthparents never
expected to see their child again. This was called closed
adoption. This was extremely hard for the birthparents.

Adoption is changing rapidly. Today, pregnant women
and their partners considering adoption may choose the
people who will parent their child. They may meet these
people. Together, they may agree that the birthparents may
see their child occasionally. They may exchange letters and
pictures throughout the years. This is called open adoption.

During pregnancy, you and your partner need to make a
plan. For many, this is a parenting plan. For others, it is an
adoption plan. Either way, you plan for your child's future.

Father's Rights in Adoption

Adoption laws vary from one state to another. In
Canada, each province has different adoption laws.

The birthmother must sign the adoption papers. The
birthfather generally must also sign them.

Usually, the adoption can proceed if the father signs *one*
of these papers:

Father's Legal Options

1. He gives permission for the adoption.
2. He denies he is the father.
3. He gives up his rights to the child.

What if your partner decides on adoption and you decide
not to sign anything? State laws vary. If you don't sign, the
adoption may take longer or it may not happen.

Birthfathers need counseling, too. You need a chance to discuss your feelings. You might realize adoption is a loving choice. You might decide this is the best choice—

- for you.
- for your partner.
- for your child.

You can learn more about adoption by talking with a counselor at either a licensed adoption agency or an independent adoption center.

Your Emotional Support Is Vital

Your emotional support is important to your partner. It's probably the most important thing you can offer right now.

Most women are easily upset during pregnancy. This is caused by hormonal changes.

It doesn't matter whether the pregnancy is planned or not. No matter what her age, these hormonal changes are very real. If she seems crabby, be patient.

Your partner may have other problems. Her parents may be upset about the pregnancy. It's hard for her to continue her education. The future may look pretty scary. Your support can help her deal with these feelings.

You also may feel a lot of pressure and confusion about your situation. Try talking to a knowledgable adult you trust. This may help.

The fact that you're reading this book means you're taking the steps necessary to help make things better, and the next chapter suggests ways you can be involved in parenting your child long before he is born.

When you're there during pregnancy, *you're getting an early start on parenting.*

You can encourage her to eat foods your baby needs.

CHAPTER 3

Parenting Starts With Pregnancy

My life changed a lot during pregnancy. We stopped going out so much and mostly stayed home.

She had morning sickness 24 hours a day. Once she did feel good, she was gigantic pregnant and had to go to the bathroom all the time. I knew what was going on, and I figured we had to take it day by day.

Greg, 17 - Liana, 1 year (Nicole, 17)

Parenting starts with pregnancy. You and your partner can do a lot to help your baby be born healthy and strong.

She should be seeing the doctor at least once a month, and more often during her last trimester. In fact, the doctor will probably want to see her each week during her last month. These visits are extremely important for her and for your baby. If you can go with her, she will probably

appreciate your support—and you'll feel closer to your
child, especially when the doctor lets you listen to his/her
heartbeat or see the ultra-sound picture.

Is She Moody?

*She's going to act different—she's going to be a lot
more moody. You need to understand that, and it's
real hard. I don't think I handled it the best.*

*You need to think about how she's feeling. The
biggest thing is they don't feel pretty, and they're
scared about the baby being born just like you are.*

*You're both going through a lot of pressure.
You're still young, too, but you need to take the
responsibility. It's the big changing period.*

Zach, 19 - Kevin, 20 months (Erica, 16)

Are you finding that your partner is moody and crabby
more often than she used to be? The hormones in her body
are changing rapidly as the baby develops, and this causes
the moodiness. She may also have a lot on her mind, and
feel she has too many decisions to make.

*She was crabbier during pregnancy. We'd see each
other three or four times a week, and we used to get
into fights a lot.*

*The father should just deal with it regardless what
mood he's in, just sit there and take it. If she do make
you mad, you should walk out and go to the park and
relax. Don't turn your back because that puts a big
hurt on her.*

Jermaine, 18 - Amy, 1 year (Angela, 17)

If you can be patient when she's moody, perhaps be
extra thoughtful, she may feel better. Try not to do anything
or say anything that will make these moods worse. Continuing depression could have a negative effect on the baby.
One thing is sure—she won't be pregnant forever!

She May Not Feel Well

Even though she's seeing her doctor regularly, your partner may not feel well at times. Pregnancy brings changes to a woman's body. Some changes are pleasant, some are unpleasant.

Many women have morning sickness during the first three months. Throwing up each morning is hard to handle. If your partner feels sick, encourage her to drink lukewarm water or herb tea and eat soda crackers.

Eating small meals more often may help. She should never use over-the-counter medicine unless her doctor says it's okay.

She's likely to feel tired much of the time. This is because her body is preparing for the baby. You can encourage her to take naps, and you can exercise with her. Taking a walk after lunch or dinner may help as much as a nap.

> *The doctor said it was good for her to walk, so I'd ask her to go for a walk. She'd say, "We have a car. Let's use it."*
>
> *I'd tell her, "We're just going to the corner store." I'd help her up, and we'd walk and talk.*
>
> Alton, 17 - Britney and Jakela, 1 year (Sharrell, 19)

She'll need to go to the bathroom more often, especially during the early part of pregnancy and during the last two or three months before the baby is born.

Your partner's blood supply changes throughout her pregnancy. Her uterus is growing rapidly, which draws more blood to her lower body. She may sometimes feel dizzy, especially if she's been standing for a long time.

If this happens, you can help her lie down with her feet higher than her head. If she can't do that, she should sit down and put her head between her knees, then breathe as deeply as possible.

Help for Discomforts

She may complain of heartburn. If so, she might try eating small meals often, avoid greasy foods, and eat more fruits and vegetables. Doing these things also helps prevent constipation, a common problem during the last weeks of pregnancy.

Her breasts may get bigger and more tender. Her breasts are getting ready to give your baby mother's milk. She may have already noticed the pre-milk, colostrum, leaking from her breasts from time to time. Some moms leak earlier than others, but when they're pregnant, all women's breasts get ready to breast-feed. Were you breast-fed?

As her pregnancy progresses, her uterus becomes bigger and presses against several organs. These often cause shortness of breath and back problems. Sleeping with extra pillows under her body may help her feel better.

If she exercises throughout pregnancy, she's less likely to have back pain. If her back hurts, heat may make her feel better although she shouldn't sleep on a heating pad.

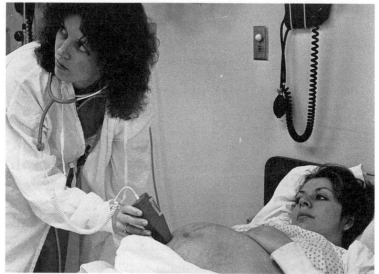

Her doctor will help her have a healthy pregnancy.

A backrub can help, so perhaps you can develop your massage skills. If she rests with her legs up, it helps both her back and her legs.

Emotional Support

It was difficult. She wanted me there all the time. If I would go to my friends, she'd get mad. I'd try to calm her down. She felt alone, and she was afraid she might have the baby early. I'd talk to her, and she'd understand. If you don't talk to her while she's pregnant, she wonders what's wrong.

Before she got pregnant, I was mostly out with my friends. Then I had to think, I've got to change for the baby. I've got to stop going out—there are too many problems where I live. That changed me a little.

Hugo, 16 - Breanna, 9 months (Marcella, 18)

She needs your emotional support at this time. She may feel fat and ugly and think you don't care. Reassure her that she's pregnant and pretty. She may need you to spend more *time* with her. This can be far more important than spending money.

She may need to talk with you about the future—your relationship or about parenting the baby. She may be afraid of the future and need your reassurance that she's not alone. Often teen dads are also afraid of what the future will hold but may not be able to admit this to anyone. Talking together may be reassuring to both of you.

Sexual activity is okay unless it hurts her. In the last months of pregnancy, the birth canal becomes shorter, and you may need to find new positions for intercourse. Sexual intercourse should stop if there's any bleeding or her water bag leaks.

Whether or not they're sexually active during pregnancy, many couples feel a special closeness during this time.

What She Eats Matters

Encourage her to eat the foods she *and your baby* need.

A mother who does not eat right could have a less than perfect baby, especially if her own body is still growing and maturing. She probably will have a healthy baby if:

- She eats foods she and baby need during pregnancy.
- She stays away from alcohol, cigarettes, and drugs including caffeine.
- She sees her doctor regularly.

You can help her do all these things.

> *When Bethann was pregnant I'd get on her case. I'd see that she ate right. I would take her to the doctor. I was like a watchdog for her.*
>
> Shaun, 19 - Troy, 2 months (Bethann, 17)

If she's like most of us, she won't want to be lectured about her eating habits. If you're together a lot, however, you can be a big influence. The foods she needs to eat now are also good for you. If you eat foods from each of the groups on the Food Guide Pyramid regularly and go light on the junk food, it will be easier for her to do the same thing. And you'll both feel better.

She also needs to drink 6-8 glasses of water each day. Water is much better than soda for her and your baby. Too much soda can cause dehydration, which can be serious.

Your Baby Eats What Mom Eats

Your partner and you need food daily from the five food groups shown in the three lower sections of the Pyramid:

Protein — Meat, poultry, fish, eggs, beans: 3 servings

Dairy products — milk, yogurt, cheese: 3 servings

Grains — bread, cereal, spaghetti: 6-11 servings

Vegetables — 3-5 servings

Fruits — 2-4 servings

If she's sick or has heartburn, eating may be a special problem. She may not be hungry at times, but she still needs to eat for the baby's sake. The baby is hungry! He must have food from the mother's blood stream continuously. If she's not sure what to eat, ask her doctor, prenatal teacher, or nutritionist.

Few of us eat a perfect diet every day. For that reason, your partner's doctor will prescribe prenatal vitamins.

Limit the Fat

Cutting back on the fat in your food would be a good idea for both of you.

Foods high in fat include:
- lunch meat, hot dogs
- desserts such as pie or cream puffs
- sweet rolls, doughnuts
- chips
- anything deep fried.

Although each mom is different, most pregnant teens should gain between 28 and 40 pounds during pregnancy.

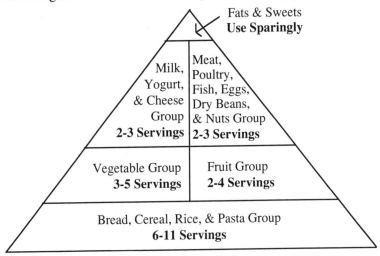

Food Guide Pyramid — A guide to daily food choices

A reducing diet at this time could harm the baby.

Pregnant teenagers often worry about gaining too much weight. If she eats a lot of junk food, she may have this problem. If she has french fries and a coke very often, she's likely to gain too much.

Instead of snacking on french fries or chips, choosing nutritious foods such as fresh fruit, peanuts, yogurt, and milk will give both of you longer lasting energy without lots of calories. These foods also give baby more energy.

The Fast Food Dilemma

If you and your partner like fast foods, you can still choose healthy items. If you decide to be a good model, for example, don't order a double bacon cheeseburger, fries, and soda. This combination is high in fat and calories and includes very little vegetables and no fruit.

Instead, try charbroiled chicken (not fried), low-fat milk, and salad. This meal provides lots of protein and a reasonable number of calories. Fat content is much lower.

Eating a lot of fast foods may mean she's getting too much sodium (salt). Pregnant women may salt food to taste, but fast foods come already salted.

Encourage her to eat the foods she needs all through pregnancy. *Your baby will thank both of you!*

Smoking Harms Fetus

When you and your partner smoke, so does your unborn baby. Even being in a smoke-filled room or car is hard on a fetus. This can cause premature delivery and/or low birthweight.

If you smoke, can you cut back, perhaps quit because of your baby? At least, don't smoke around your partner and unborn child.

Does she smoke? Perhaps you can help her stop.

If you both smoke, it helps her most if you both quit. There shouldn't be smoking around the baby.

It's hard to quit smoking, especially when you've smoked for several years. I encouraged her, and she quit cold turkey. I quit, too.

Ivan, 16 (Heather, 8 months pregnant)

The only way you can make someone stop smoking is if you stop doing it. When I knew Melissa was pregnant, I would leave my cigarettes at home.

We both quit drinking.

Raul, 16 - Adrianna, 10 months (Melissa, 20)

All three of you need good food.

Fetal Alcohol Syndrome (FAS)

Do you and your partner like to party? If you do, she may be tempted by the alcohol and drugs. Perhaps you'll decide to help her by being a good example. If you don't drink or take drugs, it will be easier for her. You don't want her to give these things to your unborn child.

Fetal Alcohol Syndrome (FAS) affects babies whose mothers drank alcohol during pregnancy. Alcohol can hurt your baby physically and mentally. Even small amounts of beer, wine, or other alcohol can harm your baby.

An FAS baby may be too small at birth, especially in head size. Unlike most small newborns, the FAS baby never catches up.

Most have smaller than average brains. This results in some mental retardation.

FAS babies are often jittery. They usually have behavior problems. Almost half of FAS babies have heart defects. These defects may mean the baby must have surgery.

Your baby's vital organs develop during early pregnancy. This is the most dangerous time of all to drink.

Drugs and Pregnancy

If mom takes drugs during pregnancy, your child can be affected all through her life. A baby exposed to drugs before she is born may be mentally retarded. She may have other problems such as:

- learning disabilities
- language delays
- hyperactivity
- poor play skills
- other conditions that interfere with normal life

Babies who are born addicted often are handicapped. An addicted baby may be taken from his mother by Protective Services and placed in foster care.

Crack, cocaine, and crystal (crank) all have the same effects. All three cause small holes in the brain and may cause the placenta to separate early.

Effects of cocaine, crack, and crystal may not be noticed at birth. The parents may think they were lucky. Problems may not show up until the child goes to school.

Pot smoking also affects your unborn baby. This reduces the baby's oxygen supply, which can cause brain damage.

Drugs sold "over the counter" can also be a problem. The right dose for mother means baby gets a huge over-dose. Some cough and cold remedies contain alcohol. These and other common medication needs should be discussed with her doctor.

You Have an Important Task

Pregnant teenagers tend to grow up fast. They must deal with the physical changes of pregnancy, and they are facing other great changes in their lives.

If you aren't close during the pregnancy, it may be hard for you to understand. Even if you're with her, you may still find it hard to deal with her moodiness. She may not be as much fun as she was. As the months go by, she may focus more and more on her baby.

> *The father has an important job during pregnancy —to support her. We'd fight a lot, but I'd never tell her she looked bad. When they're pregnant, they have real low self-esteem anyway, and you have to be supportive, completely supportive.*
>
> *If you aren't getting along, agree to disagree. Even if you've split up and don't like each other, you have a kid together. You have to support each other.*
>
> Zach

Parents who support each other are doing their child a favor.

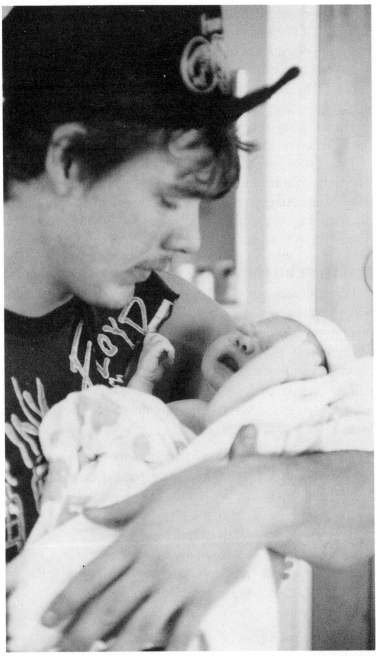

Your baby has a lot of growing to do between conception and birth.

CHAPTER 4

Baby's Development Before Birth

We all started life in the same way. Our father's sperm joined with our mother's ovum (egg) and we grew for about nine months inside our mother's uterus.

Going from conception to birth is quite a journey. It starts in the woman's fallopian tube.

Cells Develop and Divide

At first, your baby looked like a tiny ball of cells. That ball of cells grew fast as it moved down your partner's four-inch long tube.

It went into her uterus, then spent a day or two deciding where to grow. At this time, the number of cells increased quickly. This all happened before your partner missed a period.

Gestation: Measure of time since conception.

One Month Pregnant

When she's one month pregnant,
your baby is 1/2 inch long. Baby's
arms, legs, and shoulders begin to
appear. The eyes are present although the baby can't see yet. Baby's
brain cells are already developing.

*Four weeks
drawn
to actual size.*

Second and Third Months (5 - 131/2 weeks)

During the second month:

• Baby doubles in length.

• Arms and legs are barely beginning.

• The body is working mainly on the
   internal organs—the liver, stomach,
   gall bladder, and spleen.

• Tiny fingers begin to develop.

• Baby's tongue and teeth are forming.

• Baby's heart pumps blood.

During the third month:

• He is 31/2 to 4 inches long.

• His brain is growing rapidly.

• Sexual organs develop.

• Baby's fingerprints are fixed
   for life and can't be changed.

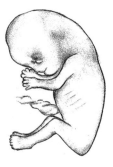

*Eleven weeks
drawn to actual size.*

When she's three months pregnant, all the parts of
baby's body have started to develop. During the rest of
pregnancy, these parts grow bigger and more efficient.

After birth, they will work on their own. They won't
need mom's blood supply to survive.

Four Months
By 16 weeks:

- Baby is four to five inches long.
- Muscles and skin of baby's face now reflect those of her parents.
- Tiny fingernails begin to grow.
- Lungs and liver are the last organs to mature.
- Baby begins to breathe amniotic fluid.

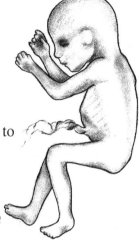

Sixteen weeks drawn to actual size.

Amniotic fluid: Water around baby while he's growing inside mom.

Five Months:
By the twentieth week:

- She is halfway through her pregnancy.
- The fetus will weigh almost 1 1/2 pounds and be about 12 inches long.
- She can feel him moving around inside her.
- He opens and closes his eyes.
- He senses light and dark.
- He may suck his thumb at times.

The doctor can easily hear your baby's heart beating now. He will check baby's heart at every visit.

Baby's ears are also developed by this time. Sometimes he moves when he hears loud sounds.

Sixth Month—Not Ready to Be Born

If your baby were born during mom's twenty-fourth week of pregnancy, he might live. He's not ready for the outside, however. If born at this time, he has less than a fifty-fifty chance of surviving.

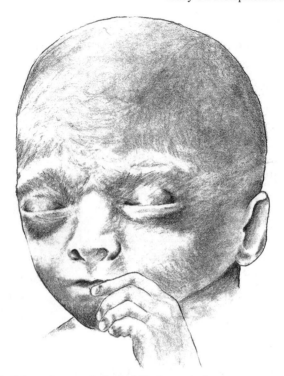

*At 24 weeks your baby is fully formed—but not yet ready
for life on the outside.*

By twenty-four weeks:
- Baby has hair and eyelashes.
- He also has fine baby hair called *lanugo*.
- Baby is covered with a creamy substance called *vernix*.
  This makes his skin soft. When your baby is born, you
  may notice it in the folds of his skin.
- Baby can now cry, but very weakly. If born at this
  time, his lungs wouldn't work well.

Checking on Your Baby

Ultrasound: A test using sound waves.
These waves show the outline
of the baby in the uterus.

Your partner's doctor may talk about an ultrasound. This is done in a doctor's office or at a laboratory.

An ultrasound doesn't hurt at all. It is done to see how baby is growing. It also predicts mom's due date. Certain birth defects can be discovered with an ultrasound. It may tell you whether baby is a boy or a girl. (It could be wrong.)

Is she having an ultrasound? If so, ask your doctor for a copy. It's a picture of your baby although it won't look much like a photograph.

Several times during her pregnancy the doctor will have blood tests done. One will show her blood type. Another is called AFP (alpha feta protein), and it measures the protein in her blood. Many doctors do this test instead of the ultrasound.

Baby Feels Crowded

Baby gains weight by making fat during the last ten weeks. She has had very little fat up to now. Fat provides energy for rapid growth. Fat also gives the body softness and curves.

Fat helps baby feel cuddly to us. It also protects baby from heat and cold.

Baby can live outside at this time. However, he is not ready to be born. If he's born before 36 weeks gestation, he will have to stay in the hospital "finishing" his development. This may take ten to twelve weeks.

Babies born too early often have problems. Some tiny babies outgrow these problems. Others do not.

At 40 weeks, the average baby weighs 71/2 pounds and is 20-22 inches long. His mother has gained at least 25 pounds during her pregnancy. Baby is now ready for life on the outside.

Your baby's journey from conception to delivery is an exciting trip.

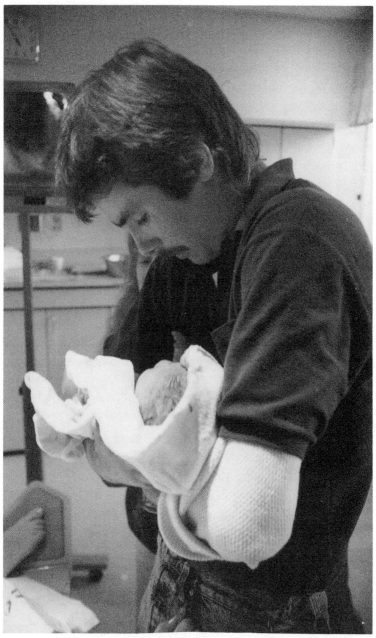

Holding your baby minutes after she's born is an experience you'll never forget.

CHAPTER 5

The Birth
Of Your Baby

Tara was in a flea market with her mom when her water broke at about 11 a.m. They called me at school, and I left. She stayed home until 1:30. Her aunt, her mom, and I drove her to the hospital.

About 8:00 that night they gave her a drug to start contractions. By 10:30 they were getting real sharp, and Alexis was born at 12:38. I was there when she was born. It's hard to describe— it's wonderful because it's part of you. Watching Tara go through the pain was the hard part.

The doctor asked if I wanted to cut the umbilical cord, and I said, "Sure." It's amazing.

When they let Tara hold Alexis, it was great. I was videotaping the whole thing.

Dennis, 17 - Alexis, 6 months (Tara, 20)

Your partner is probably thinking about labor and delivery by the time she's five or six months pregnant. Some mothers describe their baby's birth as a high point in life while others are much more negative. Each person's experience is different.

Preparing for Childbirth

Taking a prepared childbirth class with your partner is a good plan. Sign up early because the class may fill up quickly. If you can be her coach during labor and delivery, you can help her handle your baby's birth more positively. Most hospitals these days have ABC or birthing rooms, and most let the coach go into delivery with the mother. Check with her doctor.

Labor contractions used to be called pains. When she's having a contraction, it feels like her uterus is making a fist. Her belly gets hard as the baby pushes it. The contractions help push the baby out.

Contractions can cause discomfort and, for some women, quite a bit of pain. If you take prepared childbirth classes together, you will both learn the best way for her to breathe through her contractions to make labor and delivery easier for her.

She will also learn relaxation exercises that will help her prepare for labor and delivery. You can practice these exercises with her.

The prepared childbirth class helped me a lot. It showed me what to expect. I learned how to breathe, and how to pace myself. Each time a contraction came, I tried to be calm.

If you think it's going to be horrible, it will be worse. If you keep calm, it's not as painful or as hard.

Delia, 16 - Kelsey, 7 months (Randy, 17)

Prepared childbirth doesn't mean any one "method" such as Lamaze. There are several different methods. Sometimes prepared childbirth is called "natural" childbirth. This does not mean she can't have medicine to ease the pain. With preparation, however, she may need little help from drugs.

You and your partner should talk to her doctor about

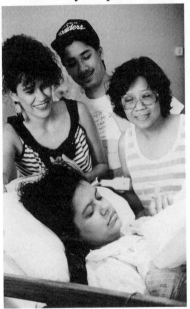

Three coaches are fine!

pain relief during labor. She needs to know her choices *before* her labor begins. Even if she doesn't want drugs during labor and/or delivery, you both should learn about her choices.

If her mom or her girl-friend (or both) want to coach her, let them share. David Crawford, prepared childbirth and teen parent teacher at William Daylor High School, Sacramento, California, says he feels three coaches are the ideal support system.

She May Have "False Labor"

During the last few weeks of pregnancy, your partner's body is getting ready for the baby's birth. Her uterus may begin practicing for this big event. She may feel early contractions. These early "false labor" contractions are called Braxton-Hicks or pre-term contractions. If she can relax and work with the baby now, she's likely to have less discomfort when real labor begins.

Some moms don't have these pre-labor contractions. Others have them off and on for several weeks. If this is real labor, her contractions won't go away.

Early Signs of Labor

During pregnancy, a woman's cervix (opening to the uterus) is sealed with a mucous plug. This plug keeps germs in her vagina from getting in her uterus. If germs could reach the unborn baby, they could give him an infection.

When this plug comes out, it's a sign that labor day is soon. Some mothers, however, never notice the mucous plug. Their labor may begin when the bag of water breaks. This is the sac that lines the uterus where the baby grows.

When this happens, she'll feel a gush of warm water. It keeps coming out no matter how hard she tries to stop it.

I came home from work at 11:30 p.m. and slept for half an hour. She woke me up and said her water bag broke. We went to the hospital—she was hurting a lot.

We called her mom, and she came to the hospital. I was so tired I fell asleep for awhile, and her mom helped. She was in labor for 101/2 hours.

Sen, 20 - Sooyung, 6 months (Marcy, 17)

For still other women, contractions are the signal that labor is beginning. Or she may have a backache and feel "heavy" when labor starts. Using prepared childbirth exercises at this time usually helps.

Role of Her Coach

You can just be there to encourage her, or you can be one of her coaches.

The coach's role:
- Assure her she is not alone.
- Comfort her. Make her feel as good as you can.
- Give her both emotional and physical support.
- Help communicate to her and from her to others.
- Remind her of the "tools" she learned in childbirth preparation class.

- Remind her of the "tricks" you remember from that class.

Be there with her *all the way*. Lend her your eyes filled with love, your smiles filled with encouragement.

Provide her with as much comfort as you possibly can:

- Lend her your hands to help take away the pain. Massage her back, feet, or wherever she wishes. Get her whatever she needs.

- Lend her as much emotional support for as long as she needs it. Communicate your feelings to her in a loving, caring, warm way. Give her your strength.

Give her the technical assistance that you both learned in your preparation class:

• Relaxation	• Breathing patterns
• Concentration	• Knowledge versus fear

- Positions for labor and delivery

You need to do only what you can do or will feel comfortable doing. No one expects you to know everything or remember what will work or not work.

If you're not sure, ask the nurse. But remember, this is the *birth of your baby*.

Timing Her Contractions

When her contractions start, you or someone else should time them. How far apart are they? Check the time from the beginning of one contraction until the next one begins. This is the *interval*.

How long do they last? Check the time from the beginning of the contraction until it stops. This is called the *duration*. Your doctor will ask about both the interval and duration.

Fetal Monitor Measures Contractions

When she arrives at the hospital, she'll go to a labor room, and you can probably go with her. The nurse will place a *fetal monitor* low on her stomach.

Fetal monitor: Machine for measuring contractions.

It shows how long, how hard, and how often contractions come. It also keeps track of the baby's pulse.

The last period of labor is called transition. Her contractions are hard and coming often. At this point, her labor is almost over. She's moving toward delivery of your baby. The baby moves down into the birth canal. He prepares to come out.

Finally—The Delivery or Birthing Room

In the delivery room, she'll be on a table. She'll be in a position like the one for a pelvic check-up. If she delivers in a birthing room, she'll be on a bed.

She may have chills. If she does, ask for a blanket to cover her legs and body. It isn't really cold. It's a hormonal change that prepares her for delivery.

After she's in position, the doctor may wash the birthing

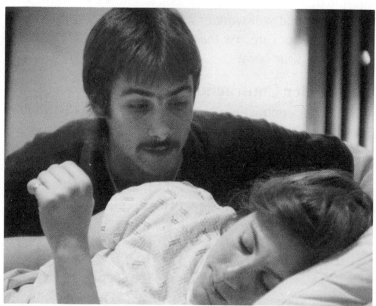

Comfort her. Make her feel as good as you can.

area. He will carefully watch the baby's progress. They will check the baby's heart rate often. Don't be alarmed if they give mom some oxygen to help the baby. They are simply making sure things go well for both mom and baby.

> *It was a long night—she was in labor 121/2 hours. It was scary at times, seeing how much pain she was in. You get to feeling guilty.*
>
> *I sat there and told her to breathe. She had an epidural, but she was awake for most of it. It was rough. I didn't think it would be that bad.*
>
> *When he was born, I felt proud.*
>
> Billy, 19 - Destini, 6 months (Violet, 17)

When the doctor or midwife decides it's time, she'll tell mom to push when she's having a contraction. This feels like the urge to have a bowel movement.

Pushing too soon may make the cervix swell. This can slow things down. It also puts pressure on baby's head.

When the head of the baby appears, it's described as crowning. What a lovely word! Someone important is being crowned—your baby.

It usually takes less than an hour of pushing to bring your baby out. Three good pushes with each contraction are suggested. Many mothers say this is the most exciting part.

Right before delivery, the doctor may do an episiotomy.

Episiotomy: a small cut made to make
the vaginal opening bigger.

Not all women need the extra opening. Sometimes doctors make it to avoid the chance of having the tissue tear.

Your Baby Is Born

With crowning, the baby goes from mom's body into our world. The head slips out and turns to the side. Baby's shoulders now come out one at a time. Then the rest of the body comes quickly. This all takes less than five minutes!

During the later stages of pregnancy I got real scared because I started thinking of all the complications. That was the biggest scare of my life, because I wanted the baby to be all right. Then when Kevin started to come out, I was even more scared. Please don't let anything be wrong. I was so scared.

The head came out, and then the whole body. I immediately counted all the fingers and toes, then looked at which sex it was. By this time I was ecstatic. My eyes were watering. It was such an experience. The nurse laid Kevin on Erica's chest. I cut the cord, I kissed Erica, and said, "Congratulations. You did a

You can encourage her to breathe with her contractions.

good job." Then I held Kevin.
I knew then it was all worth it.

Zach, 19 - Kevin, 20 months (Erica, 16)

You and mom will feel lots of excitement. You'll find out whether you had a boy or a girl (if you don't already know from the ultrasound picture). You'll learn about the condition of your new person.

Your Newborn's Appearance

Your just-born baby may look red, wrinkled, and worried. You and his mother, however, are likely to think he's the most beautiful baby ever born.

His head may be "molded" during delivery. Instead of looking round, it may seem too long. He may have strange lumps on his head, too.

At birth, the bones in baby's head are soft. This allows his head to change shape slightly as it goes through the birth canal. Soon his head will become round again.

Whatever their ethnic origin, most babies are fairly red at birth. Some even look purplish. Within a couple of days, baby's skin will look better.

At birth, black babies' skin is often lighter than it will be later. The skin at the tip of the ear is close to the baby's "real" color.

Some babies cry immediately. Others need to have mucous or amniotic fluid removed first. The nurse will gently remove these fluids with a bulb syringe.

When your baby cries, his skin may turn red and blotchy. This, too, is normal.

The baby will sometimes come out with white cream-like lotion covering his body. This is called vernix, and it protects baby's skin during his nine months in the water. Often babies come out blue-purple in color, then turn to grey-white. Sometimes baby comes out with some of the blood from the mother on him.

Delivery of the Placenta

The delivery of the placenta or afterbirth completes the birth process. The placenta has fed your baby for nearly nine months. It now separates from the uterine wall and comes out. This happens within 15 minutes of delivery.

The doctor then repairs mom's episiotomy with a few stitches. Large sanitary napkins are put on her. She'll have a very heavy period-like flow of blood for a few days.

For Some, a C-section

Caesarean section (C-section): Birth of child by cutting through walls of abdomen.

She had preterm labor and the toxemia got pretty bad to where it endangered the baby. She stayed in the hospital for five days before he was born.

During this time I was scared. I couldn't help her. Her blood pressure was up, and it was a hard time.

She had a C-section because he was breech.

Daric, 16 - Kianna, 1 year (Kim, 18)

About one in five moms has a Caesarean section. Reasons for doing a C-section include:

- The baby is too big compared to the mother's size (called "fetal pelvic disproportion").
- Labor slows down or stops.
- Certain types of infections occur such as herpes.
- Placenta previa (placenta covers inner cervix).
- Fetal distress (baby is in danger) or maternal distress (mom is in danger).
- The position of the baby is a problem. It may be breech (bottom first) or transverse (sideways).
- Failure to dilate enough for baby's head to go through birth canal (called "failure to progress").
- Prematurity

Your Baby's First Test

The nurse will measure your baby's responses. This test is called the Apgar score. It's given to baby right after he's born. He'll be tested again after a few minutes. Scores range from 0 to 10. Most babies score between 6 and 9.

The Apgar test measures:
- color
- pulse
- cry
- movements
- strength of breathing

The nurse will weigh and measure your baby and wrap him in a blanket. She may give him back to you for awhile. She may then take him to the nursery for observation. You can probably go with your baby to the nursery.

I remember just looking at her. This is so weird, this is part of me, this is ours. It was scary though, because I realized I had something depending on me. It was scary. All my life I depended on someone else. I still was, and now somebody depended on me.

Zach

Your life has changed!

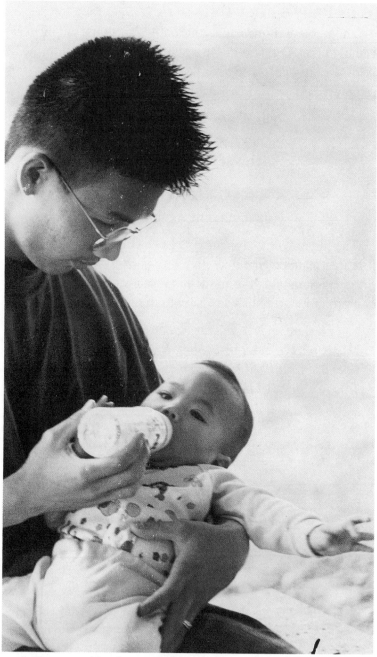

No propped bottles ever! Baby needs your love while he eats.

Caring
For Your Newborn

*Those first two months are frustrating because they
cry. I'd try to feed him, and he wouldn't eat, and I'd
get more frustrated. You have to realize it's going to
be like that. You have to be real strong in the mind
and keep your cool. It's real hard.*

*I wasn't able to sleep because every 15 minutes I'd
have to stand up and check on Braxton that first week.
They don't sleep quietly—they don't even sleep.*

*In the middle of the night Susanne wouldn't wake
up. She would cover herself with a pillow—it was too
much for her. It would make me mad because she
wasn't strong. I felt like she wasn't doing enough, like
she had the baby and she didn't care any more.*

*I'd sit down with Braxton, and I'd hold him. I'd
sing to him and play my guitar. For awhile it was*

*a problem because I wasn't getting enough rest. I
missed a lot of school.*

Antonio, 16 - Braxton, 4 months (Susanne, 15)

Those First Days

Both you and your partner will probably be very tired
the first few weeks after your baby is born. You'll lose
sleep when the baby is awake at night. And your partner
will be even more tired because of the hormonal changes
going on as her body returns to its non-pregnant state.

If she had an episiotomy, her stitches will hurt for a few
days after delivery. She'll have a discharge called lochia for
two to six weeks after the baby is born.

Partly because of her hormonal changes, she may feel
sad part of the time during those first weeks. This happens
so often that doctors label the condition post-partum
depression or after-baby blues.

The best cure for after-baby blues is help with child care.
Encourage your partner to do something for herself. Better
yet, can someone else watch the baby for an hour or two
while the two of you go out together? Or the three of you
could get out and do something together as a new family—
perhaps go to the mall or visit friends.

Your Relationship with Your Partner

Have you wondered what sex will be like after childbirth? You may wonder how long you have to wait. Your
partner may worry about whether it will hurt. She may not
want to do it very soon. She may be so tired those first
weeks after delivery that she has no interest in sex.

Couples generally are advised to wait for the six-week
checkup before having intercourse after childbirth. Her
vaginal tissue may still be tender the first few times. Each
of you needs to be patient with the other.

If she's breast-feeding, her breasts may be sensitive, and she may not want them to be touched as much.

The vaginal opening will be about the same size it was before she got pregnant. At first, juices that help keep the area moist may not be working well. A lubricant such as KY jelly will help.

It's very important to remember that four weeks to six months after delivery, the mother's first egg will be released without warning. This happens *before* her first regular period has arrived. Therefore, she can get pregnant the first time you have sex. Make sure you're protected!

Getting to Know Your Baby

Those first months I remember waking up in the night. We'd have times when it was my turn to take care of her midnight-2 a.m., and from then it was Aracely's time. Yvette would wake up almost every two hours. I changed her, and I shared her care a lot.
Sergio, 17 - Yvette, 11 months (Aracely, 17)

The most important part of caring for your baby is getting to know her—bonding together as closely as possible. Bonding with your baby can be described as falling in love.

When you put your finger across your newborn baby's palm, she'll grab it firmly. She seems to be saying, "I need you so much." You'll feel a tug at your heart strings.

If you interact a lot with baby—hold her, talk to her, carry on conversations whenever she's awake, you'll find the bonding happens just the way it should.

If you haven't had much experience with tiny infants, let your partner show you how to diaper, feed, and rock baby. With practice, you'll feel confident.

We shared the night feedings. Luckily Dustin started sleeping through the night real soon. We did it all together.

I don't think it would be fair if I just said I'm not getting up, I'm not going to give him a bottle. We shared the responsibility of having him. I think you have to go 50-50.

Mark, 22 - Dustin, 2½ (Kelly Ellen, 20)

You are your baby's first and most important toy. She will stare into your eyes for a long time. Remember that self-concept is developed by how people respond to us. Both you and baby's mom lay the foundation for that development.

Mom May Choose Breast-Feeding

Many young mothers and dads choose breast milk for their babies. They know this is the best possible food for their baby:

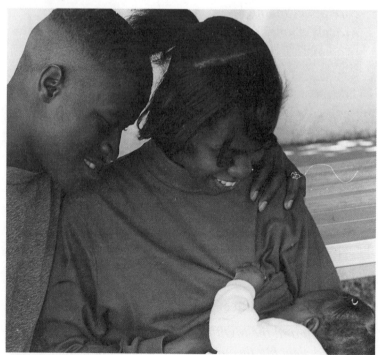

Baby's favorite food is mom's breast milk.

- No waiting
- Easier to digest

- Protects baby against germs
- Tastes better to baby

It's also easier for mom and dad—no bottles to sterilize, no formula to mix, and no bottles to heat. This can make life simpler for a tired new mother. Breast-feeding is also cheaper than buying formula.

A breast-feeding mother needs to take good care of herself. She should continue eating the same good foods she needed during pregnancy plus drink extra liquids.

Breast-feeding is likely to work better for mother and baby if baby is given no bottles during the first month. By the second month, however, give baby a bottle once in a while. There may be a time when mom won't be with her, and she'll need to know how to take a bottle. Giving her a bottle gives you a chance to feed her.

You can give the baby her water bottle, occasional formula, or breast milk pumped out by mom for later use. Some breast-fed babies would rather take a bottle from dad than from mom. They associate mom with breast-feeding.

You can do the burping. You can put her to sleep in your arms after she's eaten.

You can bathe her—or perhaps you and mom will make those first baths a team project. You'll also share in the comforting when baby is unhappy. In fact, whether or not mom breast-feeds, you'll find lots of ways to bond with your infant.

The first time I had to change him was an experience I won't forget. I had never changed a baby before. It was weird because I never had to watch over anyone, something so small that was mine. Before I hadn't even worried about myself, and now I have to give him a lot of my attention.

Andy, 17 - Gus, 5 months (Yolanda, 15)

Changing your baby can also be fun. This is about the only time a newborn is awake, aware, and not eating. Your baby is learning a lot about her world. Make sure that during those early days she sees your face and hears your voice as often as possible.

Warning

Never leave baby alone on a changing table, bed, or other off-the-floor surface for a second. The baby who couldn't turn over yesterday may be able to do so today.

We usually change him on the floor because
he's rolling now. We don't put him on tables at all.

Bill, 19 - Billy, 6 months (Jan, 17)

Bottle-Feeding Is Okay, Too

If you and mom prefer to bottle-feed, that's fine, too. Lots of babies do great on carefully measured, carefully sterilized formula. To make formula, simply follow the directions on the package or can of formula. For awhile, baby will probably prefer his formula heated to body temperature.

Heating baby's bottle in the microwave oven is a dangerous practice. While the bottle may feel cool, the formula inside could be hot enough to burn your baby.

Whether or not mom and the baby are receiving financial help from Welfare, they might be eligible for help from WIC (Special Supplemental Feeding Program for Women, Infants, and Children).

Call your Public Health Department for information. They may be able to get coupons for certain foods mom needs if she's pregnant or breast-feeding, and for formula for baby if he's bottle-fed.

The Food Stamp Program helps extend food dollars for eligible families. Ask your social worker for information.

How Often Will She Eat?

How often should baby be fed? Whenever she's hungry! Babies can't tell time yet. They need to be fed when they're hungry, and their hunger pains have nothing to do with the clock. And they *don't* cry to exercise their lungs!

At times, baby won't finish her bottle. You don't need to worry—she probably wasn't as hungry as usual. Her appetite will vary from feeding to feeding. "Enough" at one meal may not be enough next time.

Offer your baby a bottle of water occasionally, especially in hot weather. Use bottled water or water you've boiled and cooled. Don't add sugar.

No Propped Bottles—Ever

Whenever you give your baby a bottle, *always* be sure you hold him next to you. Don't ever lay him down and prop his bottle in his mouth, then leave him to drink alone.

First of all, he needs the love and emotional support he'll feel from being in your arms or his mother's.

Second, many ear infections are caused by baby drinking from a propped bottle. The passageway from the ear to the throat doesn't drain well in infancy. Milk, if not "served" properly, can go back to his ears and cause an infection.

Third, a propped bottle is dangerous for infants. Baby could choke from his milk coming too fast from that propped bottle. He could also choke on milk curds if he should spit up. He might be unable to clear his throat.

Some babies need burping several times during a feeding while others don't want or need their meal interrupted. Several burping positions work:

- Hold him upright against your shoulder.
- Support him in a sitting position on your lap.
- Lay him on his stomach across your knees.

Whichever position you choose, rub or pat his back gently until he burps. For many babies, this happens fairly quickly, while others need several minutes of help with the important job of burping.

Babies need a lot of sucking, sometimes more than they get from the bottle or breast. It's okay for baby to suck on his fist or thumb. And it's okay to offer him a pacifier. Just don't substitute the pacifier for the attention, food, or diaper changes he wants and needs when he's crying.

Infants Don't "Spoil"

You ask, "Should I pick her up when she cries? Won't she think she can get whatever she wants by crying?"

This old idea simply isn't true. Yes, she'll cry when she

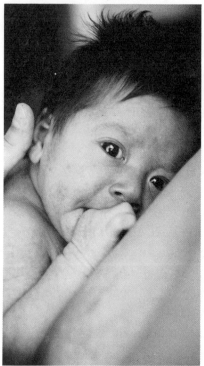

needs something. She will also learn from the parent who answers her cries. She'll learn a basic sense of trust in her world. That sense of trust is the most important thing she can learn during her first months.

When Breanna cried, I'd pick her up, walk around with her, give her her bottle. When I'd stand up with her, Breanna stopped crying. She still likes me holding her. That felt real good when she'd quit

Babies don't spoil.

crying when I picked her up. She knew she was safe in my arms.

Hugo, 16 - Breanna, 9 months (Marcella, 18)

Most parents love holding their baby. Touch her, love her. Don't worry about spoiling her in these early months. Babies under six months of age don't cry because they're spoiled. They cry because they need something, and crying is the only way they can "talk" to you. Have you noticed how her cries sound different depending on what she seems to need or want?

Even if you've fed and changed her, and you know she's neither too warm nor too cold, she may still cry. Often it's because she's lonely. Or she may be a colicky baby who just cries more than some babies do. Nearly every baby loves to be touched, held, and cuddled. Your baby snuggling into your arms makes both of you feel good.

When baby is fussy, hold her upright. Put her head near your shoulder. When she's there, she can hear your heart beat. This may quiet her. It may even put her to sleep.

Important Note

Sometimes you'll do everything you can to help your baby be comfortable, and he'll still cry. Always remember he is *not* crying to upset you. He isn't crying because you've spoiled him. He's crying because it's the only way he can tell you that he wants you.

Perhaps taking him outside will help. He may stop crying if he has something new and different to watch. A ride in the car (safely secured in his car seat) may calm him. Some parents report their babies fall asleep almost the instant the car starts.

Some babies go to sleep most easily when they're in their swing. Soft music might help. A little music box beside their bed soothes some babies.

Sometimes your baby will cry because he doesn't feel well. Is he feverish? Is he teething? See Chapter 9 for more about caring for baby when he's not feeling well.

If your bottle-fed baby cries a lot, perhaps his formula isn't right for him. Talk with your doctor. Perhaps s/he will suggest a different formula.

As you get to know your baby, you'll find still other ways to help him be more comfortable.

I go to a parenting class, and the teacher said when you place a baby on your bare chest, she'll stop crying. I tried that, and it worked.

Jamal, 16 - Valizette, 16 months (Shawnteé, 17)

Try Jamal's suggestion when your baby is crying. Feeling your skin against his may soothe him and make him feel better.

Babies and Colic

Some babies cry and cry, and it seems impossible to comfort them. Such a baby may have colic. If he does, he may seem to have a stomach ache and have attacks of crying nearly every evening.

His face may suddenly become red; he'll frown, draw up his legs, and scream loudly. When you pick him up and try to comfort him, he keeps screaming, perhaps for 15 to 20 minutes. Just as he is about to fall asleep, he may start screaming again. He may pass some gas.

No one knows what causes colic. It generally comes at about the same time every day. During the rest of the day, the colicky baby will probably be happy, alert, eat well, and gain weight.

If your baby seems to have colic, check with your doctor to see if anything else is wrong. If not, make sure baby isn't hungry, wet, cold, or lonely. During an attack of colic, holding him on his stomach across your knees may comfort him. Sometimes giving him a warm bath helps.

The good news about colic is that baby will grow out of it by the time he is about three months old. In the meantime, he will be harder to live with because of his colic. Comfort him as best you can, and look forward to the time his colic ends.

Dealing with Diaper Rash

Change your baby often. Wash her with clean water when you change her. The main cause of diaper rash is the ammonia in the urine coming in contact with air. If she gets a rash, it's even more important to wash her thoroughly each time you change her.

You can put cornstarch or baby powder on her bottom after you take off her wet diaper, but it isn't necessary. If you use baby powder, don't shake it directly on baby.

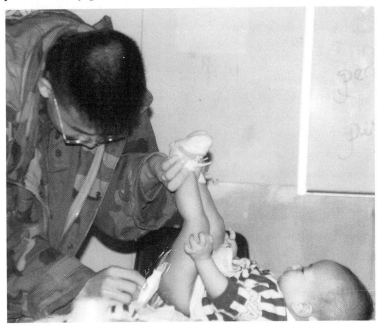

To prevent diaper rash, change her often.

Instead, put a little in your hand first, then pat it on the
baby. Baby powder shaken in the air can hurt baby's lungs.

There are both prescription and non-prescription remedies for diaper rash. You can get these either as powder
or ointment.

During the day the powder is better because, each time
you change her, you can wash it off without irritating the
rash. At night, however, when baby will sleep longer, use
the ointment. It will give longer protection.

It's easier to prevent diaper rash than it is to get rid of it.
For your baby's comfort—and your own—change her
often. And you need to clean her thoroughly each time you
change her.

Can You Take a Parenting Class?

Is there a parenting class at your school? Or does your
adult school offer evening classes on infant care? Attending
a good parenting class will help you feel more confident as
you care for your child.

> *Fathers need to get into classes like this so they
> can really know about the baby. Some men, when they
> find out she's pregnant, leave because they don't
> know nothing about it. If they learn what it's like,
> they're more likely to stay.*
>
> *This baby will be part of your life until you die, and
> you need to know what you're doing.*
>
> Agie, 18 - Mia, 1 month (Shalaine, 18)

If possible, you and your baby's mother should attend
parenting class together. Many schools offer classes
especially for school-age parents.

Some of the young men quoted in this book attend such
a class. They talked about learning how to care for their
babies. They also find support from the other young parents
in the class.

Staying Involved with Your Child

More and more fathers are realizing how much better their relationship with their child is if they're deeply involved in caring for that child from the start. They know that if only mom takes care of the baby, dad misses out.

If you don't live with your baby and his mother, you still need to be as involved as possible in his care. Make the most of the time you have with your child. Change him, feed him, rock him, play with him, and enjoy him.

If mom doesn't seem to want you to see much of your child, talk with her. Sometimes it's hard to communicate feelings about something as important as parenting your child. You're more likely to be heard if you:

• Talk when you aren't upset.
• Keep to the subject—the welfare of your child.
• Don't get sidetracked into fighting with each other.

Your baby's mom may not understand how you feel. It's important that you speak up—in a friendly way—and tell her how important parenting your child is to you.

Whether you're with your baby's mother or not, you and baby will be ahead if you're involved in baby care. When you are, everyone wins. Mom will have some of the help she needs with baby. The more you do with baby, the faster you'll bond with your child. Your baby wins by having two loving parents.

You Have a Wonderful Challenge

The first months with a new baby offer a real challenge to his parents. Your major task is simply to meet his needs as much as possible.

As I've stressed before, feed him when he's hungry. Change him when he's wet. Talk to him and hold him when he's lonely. He'll reward you by responding to you more and more as the days go by.

You're his favorite teacher.

When He's Crawling— Watch Out!

Watching Kevin develop is the best part. I couldn't wait for him to say "Dad." He started crawling, and that was fun. He became a little person I could finally relate to.

I have custody, and his mom and I worked out a plan where she sees Kevin every other weekend. Kevin usually goes to her house. And if Erica wants him other times, that's okay.

Zach, 19 - Kevin, 20 months (Erica, 16)

By the time he's two months old, baby's world is changing rapidly. By three or four months, he sits up with support. Sitting up gives him a much better view of his world.

Babies like excitement—their version of excitement. Instead of going to sleep after he eats, he wants to play. Perhaps you'll gently tickle him, move his legs slowly up and down, or give him a variety of objects to hit and grab. He'll enjoy simple games like patty-cake and peek-a-boo.

I tickle Ariana, stand her on my legs, and I have her walk on my legs. I put her on her back and pull her legs up.

Aaron, 17 - Ariana, 6 months (Selena, 16)

Toys for Baby

Her first toys need to be big enough for her to hold easily, yet too big to put in her mouth. Her toys should be washable with no sharp edges or corners. Remove any parts that come off easily. Take out the button eyes on her stuffed animals.

By four months, your baby's curiosity is growing fast, and she wants to touch and handle everything possible.

Mom bought Braxton an aquarium, and he sits in front of it. He tries to touch the fish, and he laughs. He makes little Tarzan noises while he watches.

My mom will go "Daddy's here, daddy's here," and he looks at me with this funny grin.

People say I'm conceited about my son. Of course I am. He's wonderful.

Antonio, 16 - Braxton, 4 months (Susanne, 15)

An inexpensive cradle gym is a good purchase now. It should have simple objects that baby can hit, pull, and handle. If she has a mobile, the best kind is one she can reach, touch, and hit. It needs to be sturdy. Some dads take classes that show them how to make these and other baby toys inexpensively. If you're interested, check with your adult school.

Balls are the best toy of all for baby. She can roll them and throw them. Once she can crawl, she can go after the ball. Soon she'll enjoy a big beach ball as well as having a wonderful time with the smaller ones. Of course she likes it best if you play with her. Even if mom plays with her a lot, your baby needs you, too.

Soft, cuddly dolls and little stuffed animals are important to all children. Most parents now seem to understand boys need dolls as much as girls do. After all, if playing with dolls is early practice toward being a parent, it must be as important for boys as for girls. Most men, as well as most women, will become parents.

Baby will enjoy going outdoors with you. If she isn't crawling yet, lay her on a blanket near you while you work in your yard. When she starts crawling, let her play on the grass. A little dirt won't hurt her. You need to watch her closely, of course.

An infant seat is a good purchase for this age. Don't overuse it, however. Baby would rather be carried in your arms or in a back or chest carrier rather than in a cold plastic seat.

If you're working on your car in nice weather, she may enjoy sitting in her infant seat watching you. Of course you'll put her on the floor or the ground. She is *not* safe in an infant seat on a table or bench.

As soon as she can sit up by herself, she won't want to sit in her infant seat. By that time, she probably wouldn't be safe in it anyway. She might be able to tip it over.

Build Trust by Responding

It's still important to respond to your baby's cries as promptly as possible. Letting him learn he can trust you to take care of his needs is not going to spoil him. Unhappy, dissatisfied, "spoiled" babies are far more likely to be babies who are already learning they can't depend on dad or mother to come when they need something.

Your baby may be happy much of the time. He giggles and laughs, mimics what you're doing, and generally has a

wonderful time throughout much of his day. But he wants
you or mom to be nearby.

>   *Crystal smiles and laughs a lot. She growls in the*
>   *morning like she's mad that people wake her up.*
>   *Usually she's real happy. She doesn't cry much at all.*
>   *She crawls everywhere. She tries to stand up, bend*
>   *over, and put something on the table.*
>
>   Morgan, 17 - Crystal, 9 months (Rebecca, 16)

Baby's Fears

Some babies develop rather strong fears. Sometimes it's
the vacuum cleaner. It might be the lawn mower or some
other loud noise. She may decide she wants nothing to do
with new places or different situations. A trip to the store
may upset her.

If it's the vacuum cleaner, you could try using it while
she sleeps. A better way is to let her look and explore the
vacuum cleaner before you turn it on. Then hold her with
one arm (lovingly, *not* scoldingly) while you clean for a
few minutes. Don't overdo it, of course, but she may accept
the noise under these conditions.

Always, whatever her age, treat your child's fears as the
realities they are. It absolutely does not matter if you know
"there is nothing to be afraid of." The fact is she *is* afraid.
You need to help her deal with her fear, not scold her.

Stranger Anxiety

By about eight months of age, your friendly baby may
suddenly refuse to look at strangers.

>   *Amy really doesn't know my side of the family.*
>   *When my uncle comes over, she just looks at him. My*
>   *grandma, Amy looks at her real weird. But she's*
>   *beginning to get used to grandma now.*
>
>   Jermaine, 18 - Amy, 1 year (Angela, 17)

He has matured enough to know exactly whom he trusts. He generally trusts the people he lives with and who take care of him most of the time. Now he doubts the others. Sometimes this is labeled "stranger anxiety."

If you don't see your child regularly and often, you may find he acts as if he doesn't know you. Be patient. Give him time. Let him come to you on his own terms.

She Listens and "Talks"

Your child needs you to help her develop language. You need to talk to her and read to her long before she learns to talk herself. Babies can understand more than you think. They just don't know how to get you to understand their brand of talking.

It's especially important now to talk about the things she knows. As you change her diaper, talk about it. As you dress her, say "Now I'm putting your shoe on your foot. Your hand goes through your sleeve." Name the parts of

As you play with him, you're helping him learn to talk.

her body as you bathe her. Talk about the toys you're
handing her.

> *I treat Katherine like a human being. I talk to her
> constantly. She babbles, and I talk back to her with
> eye contact. I read to her.*
> *I'd like to go fishing with her.*
>
> Paul, 19 - Katherine, 4 months (Kyla, 15)

If you aren't already reading to your baby, start now.
Choose very simple stories, preferably with pictures of
things she knows. At this age, you may have trouble getting
her attention.

Reading (mostly looking at pictures) at bedtime is ideal.
If she's sleepy, she'll be more willing to sit still for a story.
If she sits or lies still long enough for a story, she'll be
more likely to go to bed without a lot of commotion.

Curiosity Leads to Crawling

Your baby's natural curiosity pushes him toward crawling. He'll be delighted when he realizes he can move
around by himself. By this time, you need to baby-proof
your home. Put up or away the things he can damage and
the things that can hurt him.

If baby doesn't live with you, does he visit in your
home? If so, you need to child-proof in preparation for his
visits.

> *We child-proofed. We made sure everything was
> picked up off the floor because babies put everything
> in their mouths. Nothing that would harm Kevin was
> left out. Plus when he's that small, you have to be
> able to see him all the time. You have to keep a
> constant eye on him. You never leave him alone.*
>
> *The constant supervision was no big deal. That
> was some of our best times because I was working*

part-time and I could stay home with him all day.
Now I can't do that.

Zach

Your baby will learn more if he can crawl freely through your apartment or house. Caging him in a playpen or setting him in his high chair or walker for long periods of time means he's more likely to be bored. When we're bored, we don't learn much. Neither does a baby.

Prisons are not for babies. Some experts consider a playpen a baby-level prison.

Arranging your home so he can freely explore is part of your job as a parent. Baby will appreciate your efforts. The best way to baby-proof is to crawl through your home on your hands and knees as baby will. You'll see things from his level, and you'll realize what you need to put up or away until he's older.

I let Crystal get into things—she gets into the
cupboard, but I watch her. If she gets into things, I try
to give her something else. She always wanted the
phone, but we got her one of her own. That usually
satisfies her.

Morgan

Your Baby Starts Teething

The "average" baby (yours may be quite different) cuts her first teeth when she is six or seven months old. For some babies, teething is a painful experience. Others barely notice it. If she hurts, she may want to bite everything in sight. Freeze her teething rings before giving them to her— she'll like them better if they're cold.

You can buy teething lotion, which may help soothe painful gums. Put it on her gums a few minutes before feeding time. It may take away some of the pain so she can eat more comfortably.

Right now she's real grouchy because she has four teeth coming out all at once. She already has three on the bottom. When she starts crying, I put gel on her gums. That helps.

Hugo, 16 - Breanna, 9 months (Marcella, 18)

If your baby gets a fever, don't blame it on teething. She may fuss, she may even have a tiny fever if her teeth are bothering her. But if she has a "real" fever (higher than 101^0), she's sick. A fever indicates an infection. Call your doctor.

Guard against cavities in those little teeth from the beginning. Encourage her to drink water. It's certainly better for her teeth than are sweet drinks, and water helps rinse milk and other foods out of her mouth.

Avoid sweet foods. During this period you should be able to keep candy and other sweets almost entirely away from baby. If she doesn't know about them, she won't cry for junk foods. The same idea applies to soda and other soft drinks. Don't even give her a taste. Her teeth will thank you.

Nursing Bottle Syndrome

Even a bottle of milk can be a problem for baby's teeth. True, his teeth need lots of calcium to develop properly and to stay healthy. The best source of calcium is milk. He needs about 20 ounces of milk each day at this stage.

When he's old enough to hold his bottle, he may want to take it to bed with him. This is a problem if he keeps the bottle nipple in his mouth as he falls asleep, and it stays there. Milk dribbling into his mouth during the night keeps his teeth covered with a film of milk. Milk, nutritious as it is, has enough natural sugar in it to damage teeth if it stays there hour after hour.

Dentists see so many toddlers with rotten little teeth in front that they have given this condition a name: Nursing Bottle Syndrome.

If baby wants a bottle in bed with him, the solution is to fill the bottle with water. Fruit juice is even worse than milk because it has more sugar in it. If he needs the sucking when he goes to sleep, he can get it with a bottle filled with water or with a pacifier.

Bedtime Routine Is Important

Does your baby have a favorite blanket or stuffed animal? Encourage him to take one special thing to bed with him. Help him find the blanket or teddy bear that is part of the going-to-bed ritual. Read him a story. Then feed him that last bottle of milk as you rock and sing or croon to him. It may take half an hour for him to unwind, to relax enough to go to sleep.

If you follow the same routine with your child every night, you may find he goes to bed fairly happily most of the time. Your evenings will be more pleasant, too, if putting your child to bed is not a struggle.

Playing Together

She'll love playing with you. Because she likes to imitate, she may enjoy playing follow-the-leader. Keep it simple at first. Clap your hands, put a hat on your head, and wave your arms.

Most children this age love to play outdoors. If you don't have a grassy yard, is there a park nearby? Of course, being outside when you're one year old means lots of supervision from dad, mother, or another caregiver.

Playing is the most important way your baby learns about her world, and remember, you and mom are her first teachers. You can find lots of other ideas for playing with your child in chapters 12 and 15, *Teens Parenting—Your Baby's First Year.*

An extremely important part of parenting is having fun with your child. *Enjoy her!*

She prefers to feed herself.

Good Food
For Babies and Toddlers

Kianna eats just about everything—hamburgers, Salisbury steak, anything we put in front of her. She stayed on the baby food for about two months. Once we introduced regular table food, she didn't want anything to do with the baby food.

We just chopped regular food up instead of buying the junior food. That way she could eat with us.

Daric, 16 - Kianna, 1 year (Kim, 18)

Your baby doesn't need and generally shouldn't have solid food until he is at least four or five months old. Almost all babies get along best on breast milk or formula during this time.

If you feed your baby solids too soon, he's more likely:

• to develop food allergies

• to have digestive problems

Don't rush baby into eating solid food. Take your time, and offer only one new food at a time.

Rice Cereal First

It's time to start spoon-feeding about the time she's six months old. Start with infant rice cereal. Use the dry, iron-enriched kind that you buy in a box. Rice is less likely to cause allergies than other kinds of cereal such as wheat. Mix the dry rice cereal with a little formula, enough to make it quite thin at first. Use a little spoon—her mouth is little.

Sometimes parents mix cereal and formula together, then feed it to baby from a bottle. *Don't!* Your baby needs to learn to eat from a spoon.

An infant feeder which practically "injects" the food into her mouth is bad, too. *Don't buy it.*

Vegetables, Fruits for Baby

Start feeding baby vegetables, fruits, and their juices sometime between his fifth and seventh months. Mashed banana is often one of the first foods given to baby. Most babies like it, and it's super-easy to mash to a smooth consistency.

At first, offer baby only one new food each week. If he's allergic to that food—if he gets a rash or seems to have a digestion problem—you'll know that particular food is probably causing the problem. If you fed him a new food each day, you wouldn't have any idea which one you needed to remove.

She Likes to Feed Herself

Your baby can probably:

• Hold and gum a teething biscuit by five months.

- Handle little pieces of hard-boiled egg yolk (no egg white yet) by six months.

- Eat dry unsugared cereal, soft toast, French toast, cooked carrot and potato pieces, peas with skins broken, even diced liverwurst sandwiches by seven months.

She can eat all these things herself by using her fingers.

Cheerios are a marvelous early food-toy. She'll pick one up in each hand, look at it, stick it in her mouth. They contain some nutrition and, most important, are very low in sugar.

Don't give her sugar cereals. Such "cereals" should be labeled breakfast candy. Some are actually more than half sugar!

Feeding Him Table Food

If you wait until he's six months old to start baby on solid food, you'll need to use strained food for only a couple of months. He can be eating table food, much of it mashed, by the time he's eight months old. In fact, you won't need to buy jars of junior food. Feeding him from the family meals is better for baby.

He's eating about everything we eat. He likes fruits, apples and pears. We cook them and mash them up. We chop up the chicken real fine for him. Of course he drinks milk.

Tony, 16 - Felipe, 16 months (Alicia, 17)

Mash his food into small pieces. If you're serving chicken, get rid of the bone and cartilage. Then cut the meat into very small pieces for him.

She hates baby food now. She eats it very rarely. We started giving her table food at ten months—peas, cabbage, carrots, fruit. We started giving her meat

*when she first got teeth. We give her fish and ground
beef. She loves ground beef.*

*She eats when we eat plus in-between we give her
baby snacks.*

Jermaine, 18 - Amy, 1 year (Angela, 17)

Fish is excellent because it just falls apart. Of course,
you have to be very careful to get all the bones out first.

Warning

Orange juice is not recommended until baby is
about a year old. Some babies are allergic to it.

Many babies like cottage cheese. Just mash it with
a fork.

Plain unflavored yogurt is good for baby. Don't choose
the heavily sugared kind. Many children prefer the tart
flavor of plain yogurt.

The above foods, along with formula or breast milk, can
supply most of baby's vitamin and mineral needs. Iron-
fortified cereal can satisfy his need for iron. Fruits and
vegetables, of course, are good sources of vitamins A and
C. Your doctor may also want baby to take vitamin drops.

—Not the First Year—

Raw, crisp fruits and vegetables aren't good for baby
until past the first year because he might choke on them.
In fact, until he's two, if you want him to have raw
carrots, you should grate them.

When he's five or six months old, offer baby a little milk
or juice in a cup. You can buy a cup with a lid and a spout
as a bridge between bottle and cup. Before long, he'll be
able to drink a little milk, water, and juice from his cup.

Now is the time to help your baby grow into a pattern of

healthy eating that will continue throughout his life. Feeding him a variety of foods gives him an opportunity to develop a taste for different foods.

No Junk Food

If you see your child only occasionally, it may be tempting to take her candy, cola, or other junk food when you visit. Don't!

Sometimes people try to pacify a child with a sweet treat when a hug would work just as well. In fact, hugs are always better than junk food. Jello water and other sweetened drinks are in the empty calorie category too.

We don't give her cookies much, and we don't give her soda. Very little sweets, because my mom told me my cousin got a lot of sweets, and her teeth all decayed. Our doctor told us baby's teeth are real soft.

Jacob, 17 - Melanie, 13 months (Heather, 17)

Babies and toddlers need milk, water, and unsweetened fruit juices to drink—and seldom anything else.

Coffee, tea, and cola drinks contain caffeine, which is a drug. Your baby doesn't need drugs.

We give her sweets maybe once a week. We don't give her any soda because it makes her too hyper. She gets like a jet engine and gets into everything.

Purnell, 18 - Deziree, 18 months (April, 20)

You'll do her a real favor if you delay giving her junk food—soda, candy, chips, etc.—as long as possible. Your job is to help her learn to enjoy eating the food she needs to grow into a healthy, capable adult.

Baby Food—Read the Labels

If you decide to buy strained baby food, read the labels carefully before you buy:

- Choose basic fruits, vegetables, and strained meats.

- Don't buy combination meals because you get less
  protein per serving with them than you would if you
  mixed together a jar of meat and a jar of vegetables
  yourself.

- If the label tells you the food contains a lot of sugar
  and modified starches, don't buy it.

- Skip the baby desserts because baby doesn't need
  them any more than the rest of us do.

She Can Eat With You

If you're frying food for your family, it's better for your
toddler if you broil or dry-fry her food in a non-stick pan.

She can eat much of what you eat during her second year.

Serve her food before you add the spices or the rich sauce. Foods to avoid completely at this age include popcorn and nuts or any food that might cause her to choke.

He's not real picky. We eat at 6 or 7 p.m., and he eats with us. He lets us know when he's done, and we let him down.

He has sweets maybe once a week. I ate a lot of sweets when I was a kid, and your teeth suffer and your body starts to suffer. I started getting heavy and lazy. I don't want him to go through that.

Jarrod, 19 - Wade, 18 months (Valerie, 17)

Give her small helpings of food. Don't worry if she doesn't seem to eat much during the months after her first birthday. She doesn't need as much as she did six months ago when she was growing so much faster than she is now. She needs daily:

- twenty ounces of milk
- fruits and vegetables
- bread and cereal
- protein foods

If she doesn't drink enough milk, put it in puddings and soups. Does she like cheese? Let cheese take the place of some of her milk. Cottage cheese and yogurt are also good replacements.

Allow plenty of time for your toddler to eat. Rushing through a meal is not her style. She'll eat many foods with her fingers, but by her second birthday, she'll be able to handle a spoon quite well.

She'll be messy while she's eating. She may rub the food into her hair and all over her face. She'll drop some on the floor. You can put a big plastic garbage bag or a thick layer of newspaper under her chair to catch the spills.

Toddlers Get Picky

*Deziree is picky. If we aren't eating something, she
won't eat it. She has a few nights where she'll eat two
things off her plate, then get down and play. We
usually try to feed her something before she goes to
bed, like a bowl of cereal.*

Purnell

Most toddlers go through stages when they're very picky
about their food. He may eat only a few foods. It's okay to
have a limited diet as long as it's balanced. Encourage him
to eat something each day from each of the foods in the
Food Guide Pyramid. (See page 39.)

Don't try to force or even coax him to eat. Offer small
servings of nutritious food. Don't offer sweets at all. If he
seems to need an in-between-meal snack, make it part of
his daily food plan.

If he doesn't want to eat any lunch at all, calmly take his
food away. He won't starve by suppertime. Just don't tide
him over with a handful of cookies an hour later.

If he eats all his food and asks for more, give it to him
in the same way, without an emotional reaction. Whether
he eats all his food is not what makes him a "good boy."

Children who are offered nutritious food and very little
junk food tend to eat when they're hungry. If they aren't
hungry, they probably shouldn't eat anyway. So don't nag!
Instead, offer him the good food he needs, then use meal-
time to talk about what's happening today.

A toddler needs some structure at meal time. He should
be fed at about the same times each day. He also needs a
comfortable place to eat that is suitable for his small size.

He should remain seated until he's through eating, and
then be allowed to leave. Most toddlers will eat better with
some companionship. However, they should not have to sit
and wait for other people to complete their meal.

You're Her Model

Mark and Kelly Ellen were eating a lot of junk food.
When they realized that Dustin was copying their poor food
habits, they decided to change their ways. Mark explained:

> *For three or four months Dustin had cola all the
> time. He'd go through all the sodas. The same with
> Twinkies and cakes. We were drinking a lot of cola
> and had potato chips everywhere.*
>
> *Then we realized all that junk food was getting
> expensive and we were both gaining weight, so we
> started a little diet. Now we don't even buy sodas.
> Now we're real conscious about what we eat, and the
> same goes for him. For the last year or so, we won't
> give him junk food. We learned from experience. If he
> has candy all day, he gets higher and crankier.*
>
> *Junk food is like a lot of other things. If it's there
> and it's annoying, just take it away. As you take it
> away, explain why he can't have it. If we had a box
> full of cakes and cookies, he'd be into it. So we
> stopped having junk in the house.*
>
> Mark, 22 - Dustin, 30 months (Kelly Ellen, 20)

Your modeling is all important in the development of
your toddler's food habits. If you're a picky eater, or if you
survive mostly on junk food, you can expect your child to
do the same thing. If you're careful to eat foods from the
Food Pyramid groups at each meal, your child is more
likely to eat well, too.

When this happens, payoff is high in terms of your
toddler's health and general development. Her disposition
is likely to be better, too, because she'll feel better if she
eats the foods she needs.

When she's sick, she wants dad to hold her.

Health and Safety For Your Child

Deziree's been sick more than half the winter—ear infections and bronchitis. She had to go into the hospital six times for bronchial infections.

One time she got pneumonia and had to get tubes in her ears. She's been good through most of it. We can tell if her ears hurt because she plays with them. Now, with the tubes, they drain.

Usually she runs a fever when she doesn't feel good. When it gets too high, we take her to the doctor.
                    Purnell, 18 - Deziree, 18 months (April, 20)

When Should You Call Baby's Doctor?

• Baby has a temperature above 101°. Most doctors want a call if baby's fever gets this high, but check with your doctor. When does s/he want to hear from you?

- Baby gets a rash.
- Baby vomits most of his meal. Many babies spit up
  occasionally during the first two months, and it's not
  a problem. But if baby, after every feeding, suddenly
  vomits most of his meal, call your doctor immediately.
- Baby has diarrhea for 12 hours.
- Baby indicates ear pain, usually by tugging at his ear
  and/or crying.

When these things happen, call your doctor, but don't
panic.

Karina has asthma, and she came close to dying
twice. Usually we could tell when she was getting it.
No matter what, I never got real scared because when
you get scared, you panic. If you panic, you can't help
your kid.

You have to be calm and take care of her. Myndee
would freak out, and if we both panicked, we couldn't
do anything. We'd try to give Karina her medicine,
and keep her comfortable until we got her to the
doctor.

Luis, 20 - Benito, 8 months; Karina, 3 years (Myndee, 21)

Before you call your doctor, make some notes about
your baby's condition. Then you'll be able to describe his
symptoms more accurately:

- Is he coughing? For how long?
- Has he lost his appetite?
- Does he have diarrhea?
- What is his temperature?
- Has he been exposed to any diseases?
- Has he received all of the immunizations he should
  have had by this time?

If your doctor prescribes medication for your baby, ask if you should give baby all the medicine in the bottle, or should you give it only for a certain number of days?

Dealing with Fever

Fever is one of the early signs of illness in a baby, and you shouldn't ignore it. The best way to take underarm (called axillary) temperature is with a disposable or digital thermometer. These are available in drugstores. Putting a thermometer under baby's arm is less disturbing to her than is sticking a thermometer into her rectum.

What can you do about fever at home? Give the baby Tylenol or other non-aspirin pain reliever as recommended by your doctor.

Cooling baths are another way to bring fever down. If baby shivers while you're bathing her, it's too cold. A good

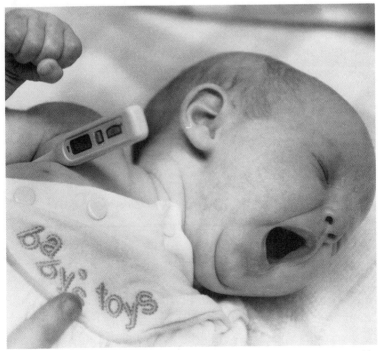

Taking underarm temperature with a digital thermometer works well.

way to do this is to put a towel in lukewarm water. Then
wrap the baby in the wet towel. It helps bring her temperature down, and she's less likely to shiver.

Lukewarm water is the best thing to use. Don't use
alcohol. The fumes can be dangerous for baby to breathe.

It's also important to give your child liquids when she
has a fever. If it's a sore throat that's causing her fever, she
may not want to do a lot of sucking. When this happens,
offer her a popsicle. It will provide some liquid.

Ear Infection? Call Doctor

He's had quite a few ear infections. He's always
playing with his ears. Once he starts pulling at his
ears, we know something is wrong. When he's sick, he
isn't himself. He's miserable no matter what you do.

Jarrod, 19 - Wade, 18 months (Valerie, 17)

When your child has an ear infection, call the doctor.
While a non-aspirin pain reliever can take away some of
the pain and the fever, it doesn't kill the germs causing the
infection in the ear. Only prescription medication can do
that, so you need to take baby to the doctor. There's a real
danger of permanent hearing loss if an ear infection is not
treated promptly.

As discussed in Chapter 6, many infants' ear infections
are caused by propped bottles.

Diarrhea Can Be Serious

Diarrhea: a thin, watery, foul-smelling discharge.

If baby has this condition for as long as twelve hours,
call the doctor. A baby with diarrhea can quickly lose a
dangerous amount of fluid.

Treat diarrhea by giving the baby clear liquids and nothing else for 24 hours. Liquids you can give him include

Pedialyte (non-prescription liquid you buy in the drugstore
or grocery store), clear water, or water mixed with apple
juice (1 tablespoon apple juice to 8 ounces of water). Offer
no solid foods, but feed liquids as often as he'll take them.

Colds Are Common

*He's had one cold. If he's sick, he just wants to be
held. We do it, it don't matter what has to be done,
dishes or make dinner, it's more important to
hold him.*

Jarrod

Neither you nor your doctor can "cure" your child's cold
—there is no known cure. You can help him be more comfortable. If he has a fever or headache, Tylenol may help.

*Ariana's had a stuffy nose like twice, and she hates
when you touch her nose. When it was runny, we put
salt water* (normal saline) *up her nose and gave her
Tylenol. After awhile she got better.*
We try not to take her out when she's sick.

Aaron, 17 - Ariana, 6 months (Selena, 16)

If she has a runny or stuffy nose, use normal saline and
a rubber syringe to clean the discharge from her nose.
Normal saline is available from the drugstore without
a prescription. The hospital probably gave you a rubber
syringe for this purpose for baby.

Decongestant medicine may also make her feel better. If
her nose is sore, cream or ointment on the area is soothing.

If she's coughing, your doctor may recommend cough
medicine. If she has a stuffy nose, a cold-water vaporizer
will help her breathe more easily. The old-fashioned steam
vaporizers are dangerous, and they don't work as well.

If she doesn't want to eat, don't worry. When she's
feeling better, she'll be hungry again. Encourage her to
drink juice, water, clear soups, even a little weak tea.

How often your child has a cold depends on two things: the number of people with colds to whom she is exposed, and her own resistance. If she's in good health generally, eats nutritious meals instead of junk foods, and gets plenty of rest, she is much less likely to get sick.

Smoke Can Cause Infection

Your child may be sick more often if someone smokes around him. Research clearly shows the dangers of second-hand smoke.

Some people find it extremely difficult to stop or cut back on their smoking. If someone in your family smokes, is s/he willing to smoke outside rather than in the house? Your child is likely to feel better in a smoke-free home.

> *Alexis had an upper respiratory infection. We took her to the doctor, and he gave her medicine.*
>
> *I'm a smoker. I don't smoke around Alexis, but the doctor said she can pick it up from my car or my clothes. I mostly smoke at work because it keeps me calm. When I come home, I change my clothes.*
>
> *She's had it twice now, the upper respiratory infection. A lot of my friends are smokers, and she's around them, too.*
>
> Dennis, 17 - Alexis, 6 months (Tara, 20)

Her stuffy nose may be caused by an allergy. Doctors usually recommend changes in diet for babies with allergy symptoms.

Some allergies are caused by plants, animals, or pollutants. Often, a baby's allergy symptoms disappear as he grows older.

> *He's been sick with lots of coughing and allergies. We use the vaporizer, and if that don't work, we take him over to the doctor.*
>
> Hilario, 16 - Cesar, 9 months (Guadalupe, 15)

Importance of Immunizations

Some illnesses you can prevent. Children used to die from diphtheria, whooping cough, polio, and other "childhood" diseases. Now you don't have to worry about these illnesses. Just make sure your child gets the DTP and other immunizations (shots) he needs.

Your Baby Will Need These Immunizations:

At 2 months	DTP, Polio, Hib, Hep B
At 4 months	DTP, Polio, Hib, Hep B
At 6 months	DTP, Hib, Hep B
At 15 months	MMR, DTP, Polio, Hib
At 4-6 years	DTP, Polio, MMR

DTP: Diphtheria, Tetanus, Pertussis

Hib: Hib Meningitis, Haemophilus B

MMR: Measles, Mumps, Rubella

Hep: Hepatitis vaccine, Type B

Call your doctor or the Public Health Department for more information on these and other shots he'll need.

Immunizations are free at the Health Department. They may be given by the Health Department at local parks or community centers. If you don't know where to take your baby for his shots, ask your school nurse for a recommendation.

Possible Reaction to Shots

Most babies have some reaction to immunizations. Usually the reaction lasts only a day or two and is mild. Giving your child a baby non-aspirin pain reliever such as Tylenol or Pediacare will help relieve these symptoms.

Of course, if your baby has a severe reaction to his immunizations (high fever for more than twelve hours or other severe symptoms), you should call your doctor.

Be sure to keep a record of your baby's immunizations. You will need these records to enroll your child in school.

Accident-Proofing Your Home

*Wade grabbed hold of a hot curling iron last week.
Every morning now when Valerie does her hair, we
have to make sure we put everything back up in the
cabinet so he can't get to it.*

*I smoke, and for awhile he was trying to grab a lit
cigarette. He runs around like a nut, and he'll fly face
first into the rocks, but the curling iron was the worst.*

Jarrod

Accident-proofing your home is absolutely essential if
you have a baby, toddler, or preschooler living there. If
your child doesn't live with you but is in your home occasionally, it's still extremely important that your place is
safe for him.

Accidents injure and kill many young children every
year. In fact, accidents are by far the greatest cause of
injury and death for this age group—thousands are
permanently crippled or killed annually.

Start with the Kitchen

*At my house sometimes I leave the skillet handle
facing out, and I'll have to change that. I'll have to
put things in the sockets and check out the kitchen. If
they're going to move in with me, I have to make it
safe. When I lived by myself, it didn't matter.*

Darrance, 17 - Jaysay, 1 year (Victoria, 17)

The kitchen is a marvelous learning laboratory for babies
and toddlers. Designing it so it's safe for your baby is an
important challenge. Hazards in many kitchens include:

• cleaning supplies (Don't keep them in the cupboard
   under your sink.)

• knives

• vegetable grater

- ice pick
- cooking fork
- hot pans (Keep the handles turned toward the back of the stove.)
- coffee pot, toaster, and other appliance cords
- iron and ironing board
- gas stove with controls baby can reach

When your child has a minor accident such as touching the stove and burning his fingers slightly, help him understand what happened. Don't say anything about "the bad stove" burning him, and don't fix it up with cookies. Sympathize, of course, but also explain that if he touches the stove when it's hot, he'll be burned.

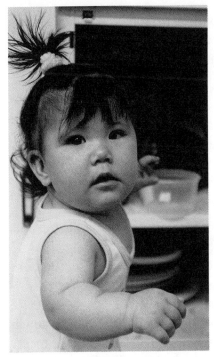

Accident-proofing your home is part of parenting.

If you ever smell gas in your home, phone the gas company at once. In most areas, they send someone out to check it at no charge to you.

Other Hazards

Water is one of the leading causes of death for children under 3. Also, babies who swallow too much chlorinated pool water sometimes suffer convulsions later.

If you live near a pool, be sure the gate is securely closed *at all times* so that toddlers cannot get into the area.

Another danger for the baby is the commonly used walker. If a baby in a walker falls down steps or tumbles into a pool, results may be deadly—much more dangerous than if he falls freely. In fact, a number of states have passed legislation banning baby walkers because of these risks.

If there is a cloth or placemat on the table, your pulling-to-stand baby will grab it. Anything setting on the cloth, whether it's hot coffee or an empty dish, is likely to be pulled down with disastrous results for your baby. Child-proof your tables!

A thin plastic bag, the kind that drycleaners use, can suffocate a baby if she pulls it over her face. Cut up and throw out such bags immediately.

Put all medicines in a cabinet and keep that cabinet securely locked.

During the time she is pulling herself to stand, be especially careful to keep the bathroom door closed. It's possible for a toddler to pull herself up by the edge of the toilet, lose her balance, fall in, and drown.

> *We put locks on the cabinet that has all the chemicals. We keep the bathroom door closed all the time. Deziree gets it open sometimes now, but usually the doorknob is loud enough so we can hear her going in. We also get up and check on her when she's too quiet.*
>
> Purnell

If you have stairs at your home, put a gate at the top and bottom to protect your creeping-crawling-toddling child.

If you have a fireplace, open heater, heating register, or floor furnace, put guards in front of and over it. Use furniture to block off radiators.

If your toddler has learned to open doors, you can attach fasteners, the hook-and-eye kind, up too high for her to reach. You'll need some method of keeping doors closed if they lead to stairways, driveways, and some storage areas.

Your window and door screens should be securely fastened. If your house has bars on the windows, they need to be the kind that can be opened from the inside.

Cars can be deadly for toddlers. If he's in the car, make sure he's buckled into his car seat. If he weighs 40 pounds or more, he can use the regular seat belt. Incidentally, be just as sure that you're buckled in, too. You're his model.

Accident-Proof Outside Areas

Yards, fenced or not, and garages need to be child-proofed, too. Check for:
- trash
- insecticides
- paint removers
- other poisons
- nails, screws, and other hardware
- assorted car parts, tools, and gardening equipment

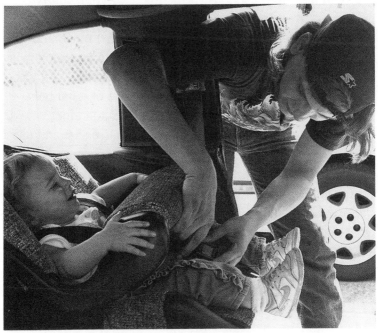

Buckle him in securely—he depends on you for his safety.

Get rid of the trash. Store the other things out of reach or lock them in the garage.

Also get rid of rusty or tippy furniture. Regularly check hammocks, swings, and other play equipment for safety.

Some plants are poisonous such as caster beans and oleander. Does your yard have shrubbery or other plants dangerous to your child? Also check any house plants in your home. Some philodendron and dieffenbachia are toxic. So are the bulbs of daffodil and other bulb plants.

Poisoning Is Big Danger

Children are most likely to be poisoned when they're ten to twenty months old. They move around a lot, explore everything in reach, put everything possible in their mouths. They aren't able to understand what's dangerous and what's not.

Cigarettes are poisonous. If members of your family smoke, ask them to keep ash trays away from your toddler.

Find the telephone number of your nearest poison control center. Keep it by your phone along with your doctor's and other emergency numbers. If you think your child has been poisoned, take any evidence you have of what he swallowed—a piece of the substance or its container.

Get some syrup of ipecac from your pharmacist and use it *if* your doctor or poison control center recommends it. It will help your child throw up. For some poisons, this is appropriate.

For others, such as toilet and drain cleaners, it's exactly what you *don't* want. Throwing up Drano will cause twice the damage because the lye burns going down and again coming up.

Is Paint Lead-Free?

Do you have furniture, walls, or woodwork in your home that were painted before 1970? If the paint contains lead, it can damage your child if he chews on the painted surface. If the paint is peeling, he may put bits of it in his mouth. Lead poisoning can be the result, a serious problem for babies and children.

> *Aviantay had to go to the doctor because she ate some paint and got lead poisoning. Her mother had to get another house because the paint was chipping off the walls.*
>
> *Monique caught it at the right time, but it really scared her. She called me and told me Aviantay was in the hospital for a day. She's all right now.*
>
> Lorenzo, 17 - Aviantay, 2 years (Monique, 18)

If children get too much lead, they show signs of lead poisoning. "Too much" for a baby may be a very little bit of the paint. The child may become anemic and lose his appetite. He may be either listless or hyperactive and irritable. He may find it harder to learn, and may suffer convulsions and permanent brain damage from the poisoning.

If you suspect lead poisoning, check with your doctor. Through a simple blood test, s/he can detect the condition. If lead poisoning has occurred, the doctor can recommend treatment to get rid of much of the extra lead in your child's body so he won't have the problems described above.

Health and Safety—An Important Challenge

Keeping your child safe and healthy during her toddler years is an important part of your parenting career. It's up to you and her mother to create a safe environment for her. It's up to both of you to care for her when she's ill. It's also up to both of you to guide her toward eating the good foods and getting the rest she needs for optimal health.

As you already know, parenting provides lots of challenges. Your reward for meeting these challenges is your child's well-being and love.

"I like the way Valizette laughs and tries to talk." (Jamal)

She's One—Soon
She'll Be Running

Now that she's a year old, Amy pulls everything off the table—a lot of stress. But regardless of what she do, that's what babies are. They get into a lot of stuff.

When she started crawling, we put child-proof latches on the cupboard doors, and gates by all the stairs and doors, and put her toys on the floor.

We put those plastic things in the sockets, and we try to keep the cords high. We're always watching her, too.

Jermaine, 18 - Amy, 12 months (Angela, 17)

I like the way Valizette laughs and tries to talk. That's what kept me thinking when I was doing my thing on the streets, I can't do that. I can't get killed or go to jail because I have a baby.

Jamal, 16 - Valizette, 16 months (Shawnteé, 17)

He Develops Rapidly

During his first year, your child develops from a helpless newborn to a whirlwind little person who scoots everywhere and will be walking soon. He can climb, and he can get into big trouble if no one is watching him.

> *My mom has those little glass things like porcelain dolls and flowers all over the place, and Roman gets into all that stuff.*
>
> *The bathroom door is always closed because he plays in the water in the toilet.*
>
> *The other day I found him on top of my computer desk. He was knocking everything off. It was funny— but how did he get up there?*
>
> *We keep putting the breakable things higher and higher but Roman keeps getting higher and higher. He stands on his little choo-choo train and climbs up on things. He doesn't walk yet, but he climbs everywhere.*
>
> Jimmy, 17 - Roman, 1 year (Rosalva, 19)

A one-year-old likes toys—form boards, blocks, balls, and stacking toys. He especially likes these toys if someone is there to watch or to play with him. Already he enjoys crayons or paints if he's allowed to use them.

> *Deziree loves to scribble. She likes finger paints, markers, and colored pencils.*
>
> *I didn't think she'd be learning this fast. She gets a learning toy, and she figures it out within a week.*
>
> Purnell, 18 - Deziree, 18 months (April, 20)

He's starting to talk through words and gestures. He can follow simple directions. His understanding of right and wrong, however, won't begin to develop until he's close to two. Even then he often won't know or understand what he should and shouldn't do.

She Copies Dad and Mom

Your toddler loves to copy you. If you're working on your car, she'll want to help. Does she have a little car to work on with you?

> *When I'm outside working on my truck, he climbs under the truck and gets full of grease and dirt. He tries to fix everything. If I'm working on something here in the trailer, he'll grab a screwdriver and try to help me.*
>
> *I love driving cars, and he loves it, too. I'll have the truck in park and shut off, and he'll stand there at the steering wheel and act like he's driving.*
>
> *He does just about everything I do. If I throw one of his balls, he'll throw it. If I go out the door, he'll go out the door. He pretty much follows me.*
>
> Jarrod, 19 - Wade, 18 months (Valerie, 17)

When you're working in the house, there will be lots of opportunities for her to mimic you. If you don't mind some water on the floor, and if you use plastic dishes, you can let her wash dishes with you.

Cooking with dad or mom is exciting for your toddler. Can she help stir cookie mix and drop spoonfuls on the cookie sheet?

If you copy her movements and her play activities, she will be delighted. Letting her know you like what she's doing is the best way to help your child have high self-esteem. This is an important part of her learning.

He Struggles for Independence

Your toddler wants to feel in control of what he eats, the clothes he wears, when/whether he uses the bathroom, and how he plays. Give him plenty of chances to make some of these decisions. If you do, he may find it easier to go along with your wishes when you can't let him choose.

Compromise and respect are magic ingredients for living with a toddler. Being sensitive to your child's need to control some aspects of his life will help you understand his behavior.

When your toddler was an infant, it was your job and his mother's job to decide what was best for him. As he grows, he will insist more and more on making his own decisions. His individuality and independence will amaze you.

Elena's very independent. Sometimes it scares me. At this age, I wonder how she'll be when she's a teenager.

When she started this, it got my attention. I would sit there and think, "Oh my god." I would go in her room, and she would literally grab me by the hand and lead me out, then close the door.

Or she would get mad at us and go in and close the door because she wanted to be alone. I guess that's okay. Her room is a safe place, and I can understand wanting to be alone. Sometimes I feel that way.

Carlos, 19 - Elena, 23 months (Monica, 18)

Dealing with Temper Tantrums

Toddlers tend to get frustrated because they can't express themselves in words very well. Temper tantrums may result. She wants to put her clothes on herself, but it's a struggle. She tries to put a square block in a round hole and it doesn't work. And she probably doesn't want your help.

She has these frustrations, and she can't talk them out. She doesn't know enough words yet so she screams. Her screaming may turn into a real out-of-control temper tantrum.

The tantrum is an expression of her feelings of anger and frustration and her inability to cope. Her feelings are sincere and strong. She is enraged and absolutely miserable. She has lost control of her behavior and may be very difficult to handle.

Losing control in this way can be scary for her. She wants to do things her way. At the same time, she needs your firm guidance. What should you do?

First, what should you *not* do? Don't spank or otherwise punish your already-upset child. If she's having a "real" tantrum, she's lost control of her own actions. If she's "just" screaming, hitting her won't help, and it usually won't stop her screaming.

Don't give in to her either. Is she screaming because you said she couldn't have a cookie right before dinner? Don't stop the screaming by handing her a cookie. If you do, what happens next time? She screams when she wants another cookie. She learns that's the way to get that cookie.

It may be best to ignore a temper tantrum. You could pick her up calmly and take her to her room, but if she's lost control, you probably don't want to leave her alone.

An even better approach may be holding her gently. Feeling the security of your arms may have a calming

She isn't enjoying her tantrum any more than you are.

effect. After all, she is a very upset little child, and she needs to know you still love her—even though you won't give in to her demands.

> *Genevieve has tantrums over the car keys. She'll have my keys, and I'll say I have to go, and I take them. She'll throw herself down and start screaming. I think I'll buy her a keyholder with fake keys that will look like my Bart Simpson holder.*
>
> Miguel, 20 - Genevieve, 18 months (Maurine, 16)

Miguel is wise to figure out a way to eliminate the *cause* of Genevieve's tantrums.

See *Teens Parenting—Discipline from Birth to Three* for more discussion of this topic.

When Your Child Asks for Help

Responding when your child asks for help is the best way to cut down on the number of tantrums he will have:

- When your child wants you, stop to see what he wants.
- If possible, provide the help he needs.
- At your child's level of understanding, briefly talk about the event.
- Once you have assisted or comforted and talked to your child, your next step is to leave him alone.

Your child learns a lot from an interchange like this:

- He learns to use another person (you) as a resource when he can't handle a situation himself.
- He learns that someone thinks his discomfort, excitement, or problem is important, which means *he* is important.
- His language development also gets a boost each time this happens.

Don't Rush Toilet Training

Toilet training is not appropriate for most children under two. They simply are not ready. Trying to teach him to use the toilet too soon only frustrates parent and child.

See the next chapter for suggestions on how to toilet train your child when he's ready.

Helping Him Talk

How can you help your child learn to talk? You already are—if you talk to him a lot. And you're helping him even more if you're reading to him.

Are there words you don't want your child to say? Then try not to have those words said where he can hear them. He learns words by hearing them—and this applies to "bad" words, too. To him, all words are interesting, and if you scold him for saying certain words, he'll have no idea why. If he says words you don't like, it's usually best to ignore them.

Now that he's beginning to talk, there are two other ways you can help him:

- Don't correct his speech, and *don't* talk baby talk to him. He needs to hear words spoken correctly. He'll learn faster if you don't criticize him if he mispronounces a word.

- Give him a chance to talk. If he points at the refrigerator, don't pour him a glass of juice immediately. Encourage him to say the word. Don't frustrate him, of course, by waiting more than a few seconds. Remember that children start talking at different ages.

If you speak two languages, help your child learn both. It might be best if one parent or caregiver always speaks one language to him, and the other parent or caregiver speaks the second language. This may help your child keep the two languages separate. By the time he enters kindergarten, he should speak both languages well.

Read—Read—Read

I've always read to him, ever since he was tiny.
He'd look at the pages when he was a month old. He
was fascinated with it.

Now he loves his books. "Book, book," he'll say.
He says, "Me read," and he makes noises.

Zach, 19 - Kevin, 20 months (Erica, 16)

If you've been reading to your child, she probably is talking more than she would have otherwise.

Choose books with bright simple pictures for your toddler. At first, she'll prefer pictures of familiar things— cats and dogs, for example.

As she grows older, of course, you won't limit her books to stories about familiar things. The rhythm of Mother Goose rhymes will appeal to her. Fairy tales and stories about animals, people, and places she has never seen are an important part of her education. Provide lots of variety in her books, because books can widen her knowledge of and interest in many different things. Books about familiar topics, however, are more likely to keep a toddler's interest.

Develop a Bedtime Ritual

Toddlers are extremely active, and they get very tired. Many resist napping. Waiting until he's exhausted before putting him to bed is *not* a good plan. He'll be less cranky if he eats and rests at regular times.

If he doesn't want to nap in the afternoon, let him take some books and a quiet toy to bed with him. Tell him it's okay if he doesn't go to sleep, but that you want him to play quietly for an hour. Some days he may go to sleep, and other times he won't. Whichever, his quiet hour will refresh him for the rest of the day—and you, too!

A baby who went to bed willingly his first year may suddenly turn into a toddler who insists on staying up. By now, he enjoys being with his parents and doesn't want to leave them. When he hits the "No" stage, bedtime may become a problem.

It's important that your child have a regular bedtime. You can't keep him up until 10 tonight, then expect him to lie down and go to sleep at 8 o'clock tomorrow night.

Starting a bedtime routine when the child is six to eight months old usually helps him settle down to sleep without a lot of fussing. At this age, it's probably as simple as holding him while he drinks his bottle, reading him a story, and putting him in his crib.

A few months later, a more complicated ritual can help prevent bedtime problems. Quiet play, a little snack, a relaxing bath, and reading helps prepare a toddler for sleep.

The important part of the ritual is carrying it out regularly. If you or mom can't be with him some nights, his caregiver needs to carry out his usual bedtime ritual.

If your child is hungry at bedtime, give him a light snack or a bottle before he goes to bed. Then brush his teeth. If he still needs something to suck on as he drifts off to sleep, give him a bottle of water or a pacifier. Either will satisfy his urge to suck.

Every-Five-Minutes Routine

If you haven't started a bedtime routine, try it. If your child continues to have a fit when you put her to bed, think about the reasons. Is it as simple as a dislike of the dark? A night-light might help.

Probably she doesn't want to be alone. She may feel deserted if you put her in bed, tell her to go to sleep, then shut her door.

If she cries and you get her up, guess what? She'll cry tomorrow night until you get her up again.

If you decide to let her cry, she may go to sleep in a few minutes. Some toddlers, however, will cry and cry for a couple of hours if left alone. They may finally go to sleep from exhaustion, but they aren't likely to sleep well after such an ordeal.

Combining the two methods (leaving her alone and giving her attention) might work. If she makes a big fuss at bedtime, explain (again) that it's time for her to go to bed. Tell her you'll be in the next room. Pat her back for a minute, tell her good night, and walk out.

If she cries, go back five minutes later, explain kindly that it's time for her to go to sleep, pat her back and say "Good night" again, then walk out. Repeat the process every five minutes until she finally goes to sleep.

She might cry for another hour the first night, but she knows you haven't deserted her. She knows you still love her. She also knows she is to stay in bed.

For the toddler who's been getting up or staying up at night, it may take a week or so to adapt to a regular bed-time. When she does, she's likely to be a happier child because she's getting the sleep she needs.

Bottle at Night?

By the time your child is a year old, he doesn't need milk in the middle of the night. If he gets a bottle at bed-time, he doesn't need more food. If he sleeps with a bottle of milk in his mouth, the risk of tooth decay is high.

If he wakes, instead of handing him a bottle, offer him a cup of water. Tell him "Good night," and walk away. If he continues crying, try the every-five-minutes routine for a week. You'll be exhausted, but if he starts sleeping through the night, you'll feel better, too, next week.

Weaning from the Bottle or Mom's Breast

If you haven't already started encouraging your child to drink milk, juice, and water from a cup, it's time to do so. If she has plenty of time to learn to drink from a cup, weaning from the bottle or mom's breast is likely to go more smoothly.

Drinking from a cup is quite different from sucking fluid from a bottle. She might like to use a cup with a drinking spout at first. Transferring to a cup later won't be difficult.

For some children, giving up the bottle is hard. Some people believe it's easier for the child (and dad and mom) if she switches from bottle to cup soon after she's a year old. She may be less willing to change if she's been sucking from her bottle for two years or more. On the other hand, some children seem to need more sucking than others.

Two things need to happen when you decide it's time to wean her from the bottle:

- She has to get enough milk—or enough calcium from other sources such as yogurt and cottage cheese.

- You and mom need to be comfortable that she's telling you she doesn't need the sucking experience any longer.

With encouragement from you and her mother, your baby may practically wean herself from breast or bottle.

She Keeps You Busy!

During her second year, your child will keep you and/or her mom busier than you ever dreamed possible. You're most likely to enjoy her if you:

- Design her surroundings so she can have as much freedom as possible.

- Give her the attention she craves.

- Set truly necessary limits, and insist she not go beyond those limits.

Good parenting is indeed an art. Your child will give you lots of opportunities to practice this art during her second year. *Enjoy!*

"When I come home from work and this little voice says, 'Daddy,'
it brings a whole new dimension to life." (Zach)

CHAPTER 11

Your Amazing Two-Year-Old

When I come home from work and I'm tired and this little voice says, "Daddy," sometimes it brings tears to my eyes. It brings a whole new dimension to life, feelings and experiences you'll never have until you're a father. It's different, and it's real neat.

Zach, 19 - Kevin, 20 months (Erica, 16)

By the time your child reaches two, he's running, jumping, and riding wheel toys. He helps dress and undress himself, and feeds himself with a little help. He enjoys coloring and painting.

He will continue to imitate your activities and those of others. He'll imitate activities you like as well as some you don't.

Simple playthings often are more inviting to a toddler than elaborate toys. If you buy a new TV, or, better yet, a big appliance such as a range, save the box for your toddler. Help him make a house out of his box. You can also throw a blanket over a card table and tell him he can play in his cave.

Plan Painting Time

Provide plenty of opportunities for your toddler to color, paint, cut paper (with blunt-ended scissors), and do other creative activities. You'll continue to supervise, of course.

Take a tip from preschool teachers and do a little organizing of your child's day. Plan a time when she can fingerpaint or paint with a brush. If the weather permits, painting outside cuts back on clean-up time.

It's best not to give your toddler a coloring book in which she's expected to color or paint between the lines. If she's at all creative, she'll have a much better time with big pieces of paper on which she can scribble as she wishes.

Let your child use whichever hand she prefers. If she's left-handed, you'll probably know by the time she's three.

How Much Television?

Research shows that aggressive children tend to watch a lot of violence on television. Research also shows that children who watch too much TV show less imagination in play and at school than do children who see less television.

A toddler who watches TV for several hours each day is missing the active play he needs. He's also undoubtedly watching shows with scary scenes, shows that give a distorted view of relationships between men and women, and other situations that tend to scare or confuse him.

We don't want Elena watching horror films. In fact, I don't think a child should watch that much TV. It's not good for their development. There's too much violence, and it can pollute their minds.

Carlos, 19 - Elena, 23 months (Monica, 18)

Can you watch TV with your child and talk with him about what he sees and hears? If the two of you watch an hour or so of carefully selected shows a day, and talk together about it, TV may have a positive influence on your toddler.

If your family watches a lot of TV, you may have little choice in the number of hours the set is on each day. Probably the best tactic in this case is to find a quiet place where you and your child can play away from TV.

Playing Outside

> *I saw Karina yesterday. We go crazy. We wrestle. We go to the park, and we went to Disneyland last month.*
>
> *I've taught her how to swim.*
>
> Luis, 20 - Benito, 8 months; Karina, 3 years (Myndee, 21)

Toddlers enjoy playing outside. It's good for them. They are usually more active outside than inside. The exercise helps their motor development. It also gives them a better appetite and makes them more ready for bedtime.

Do you have a fenced-in yard where your toddler can play? If so, she—and you—are lucky. Of course she'll still need lots of supervision.

If you don't have a yard, can you take her to a nearby park? She'll also enjoy going for a walk with you. It won't be the kind of walk where you get lots of exercise from walking fast. Your toddler will be in no hurry. Instead, she'll explore all sorts of things along the way.

Giving your child a lot of new experiences helps her learn about her world. Take her to the airport to watch the planes landing and taking off, to the train station, and to a construction site. She'll have a great time, and these are things you can do together whether or not you live with your child.

How Much Rough-Housing?

Rough-housing is an activity that toddlers and parents, especially dads, often enjoy. It's not smart, however, to play at hitting each other if you don't want your child to hit other children. Neither is it wise to get your child so excited that he'll have trouble calming down.

> *I think parents set the pace. My husband likes to play rough. Then he gets tired and wants to stop, but the kids aren't ready to stop. You can't just all of a sudden stop. You have to start going slower and taking it easier. It took him awhile to learn that.*
>
> Annabel, 26 - Andrew, 10; Anthony, 7; Bianca, 5; Brooke, 2

Active play usually is not a good idea at bedtime. You want your child to slow down. That's why a bedtime routine including a story time works best.

"Where Do Babies Come From?"

Your toddler may start asking questions about sex. If he does, let him know you appreciate his questions, then answer in terms he can understand. When he asks, "Where do babies come from?" you might say, "Babies grow in a special place in the mother's body."

If he asks how the baby got inside the mother, you can tell him that a mother and a father make a baby together. You might explain that the father's sperm gets into the mother through the father's penis.

Sometimes little girls wonder why they have no penis, and little boys worry that their penis might come off. Explain that boys and girls are made differently. Teach your child the correct names for his/her genitals. Name them as you name other body parts.

All little boys and girls handle their genitals. When they do, and find that this feels good, they may masturbate. This does no harm. It is normal, and you would be wise to ignore it.

A parent who tells his/her child that masturbation is bad may cause the child to feel naughty, or to think that sex or sexual feelings are bad. That's not a very realistic or healthy approach.

She's Learning Rapidly

Your two- to three-year-old is busily learning new words and is more able to talk. She usually understands what you tell her if you use simple words and short phrases. There will be many times, however, when she doesn't interpret the meaning correctly. To her, words generally have very simple meanings and uses. She has just barely begun to learn about language.

Often when a toddler seems to behave defiantly, she simply doesn't understand how she's expected to act. You can help her if, before speaking to her, you stoop down and get eye contact with her. Now you have her attention. Talk to her slowly and use words you know she understands.

He'll learn faster if he feels secure in your love.

Father-Child Time

*I feel a father should be involved because your
child is only young once. Once they grow up, you can
never ever get that back. You should spend as much
time with them as you possibly can. By doing that,
you see your child progressing, and you don't miss
out on her life.*

*My family is more important than anything else in
my life. My job can come and go, but every year my
child gets older, and I will never get that back.*

*Me and Elena, we have our time together. I try to
spend as much time with her as possible. But sometimes when I'm working, I'm exhausted when I get
home. She will run around and say, "Daddy, daddy,"
and I'll sit there comatose. But I like to play with her,
and she likes it, too, or I read her a story. She
loves books.*

Carlos

You're probably tired when you come home from work.
You may have little energy left for playing with your child.
However, most children look forward to a special playtime
with their dad. When this happens, a bond develops between father and child that brings pleasure to both. This
bond is the best possible basis for good discipline. If you
don't live with your child, it's even more important to plan
special times with him.

What About Toilet Training?

Toilet training should seldom be considered for children
under two. Most children aren't ready to use the toilet until
after their second birthday. Some are quite a bit older.

Attempts at early toilet training must seem strange to a
child. Imagine you're a toddler. Your parents put diapers
on you for months. They change them when you get them

wet or messy. Then one day they put another kind of panty on you, and suddenly it's an "accident" if you get those panties wet or dirty. Confusing.

You'll save yourself and your child a lot of frustration if you cheerfully diaper him until he decides he wants to use the bathroom.

Actually, successful toilet training depends much more on development than guidance. He won't be able to urinate or defecate reliably in a potty chair or toilet until he can recognize his need to go. He also needs to develop some control of the muscles that control the release of urine and BM (feces). Training him to sit on a potty chair before he's ready is quite meaningless, a waste of time for both of you.

Punishment Doesn't Help

Don't punish your child for accidents. Toilet training can't be forced. A child who feels pressured will be tense and unable to urinate when he chooses. He will be even more likely to have accidents.

When your child has an accident, calmly clean it up and put clean clothes on him. He has not misbehaved; it was an accident, and he should not feel ashamed.

When he is successful, praise him. Tell him how happy you are that he was able to do that. It will help if other family members let him know they're proud of him, too.

The ideal way to teach your child how to use the toilet is through modeling. You show him how. If you encourage your child to sit on his little potty chair while you're on the big toilet, he'll get the idea faster.

Even after training has been going quite well, some children start having frequent accidents again. If this happens to your child, don't be concerned. Handle the accidents calmly. If they occur too often, you may need to put diapers on him until he seems ready to try training again.

Some children train quite easily while others have a
more difficult time. Because every child is different, there
is no one sure method or any particular age that is best for
all children. Your child will train when he's ready.

If your child spends much time in a daycare center, or
with grandma or another caregiver, it's important that you
all work together with him when he's ready to go to
the toilet.

If You Live Apart

If you aren't living with your child, do you see her
often? Always be sure, if you tell her you'll be over tomorrow, that you are there when you said you'd be there.
Sometimes single mothers complain that their child's dad
doesn't show up when he promised he'd be there. This can
be very disappointing to a child.

Children need to be able to trust both parents. Trust goes
away when the parent says s/he will do something with the
child, then doesn't carry through on that promise.

If your child's mother doesn't want you to see your
child, what can you do? Unless the court says otherwise,
you should have the right to spend time with your child.
Perhaps if you're dependable in your visiting—let her
know when you're coming, and always follow through with
your plans to spend time with your child—she will
cooperate.

*I go over there every week. Every other week I
bring Erica home for the weekend. I talk with her,
and I play with her. I read little books to her when she
goes to bed, and she goes to sleep. I sit there with her
for awhile to make sure she doesn't wake up.*

*I like to take her to the park and walk around with
her. I take her other places too.*

Larry, 19 - Erica, 6 months (Priscilla, 17)

If You're Gone for Awhile

> *I've been in jail for two months and I get out next*
> *month. I hope we can spend a lot of time together.*
>
> Larry

If you're away for awhile, whether in the armed services,
jail, or for some other reason, it's hard to stay close to your
toddler. Encourage his mother to send you photos of him
and to describe his activities to you. The more aware you
are of your child's development and of his activities, the
more possible it will be to renew your relationship with him
when you can be together again.

Toddlers love to get mail. If you aren't with him, write
to him *a lot*. Write short letters. Tell him that "Daddy loves
you and wants to hold you in my arms." Identify yourself
as "Daddy" at least three times in each letter so that he
hears that special word. Write often.

Remember that whoever takes care of him and reads
your letters to him usually calls you by your first name or
nickname. You can help your child know you as "daddy"
through these "daddy" letters.

Send your picture to him, date it, and sign it, "With love
to _____, Daddy." It can be put on the refrigerator where
he'll see it often.

If it's possible to telephone him, do so. Even if he can't
talk yet, he'll hear your voice and associate it with the word
"daddy" and your picture.

Your Toddler's Amazing World

The whole world is fantastic to your toddler. Everything
is new. Toddlers really don't need Disneyland because they
can find excitement wherever they are. Your job is to share
his excitement, and to guide and support him as he
discovers his world.

Discipline for infants and toddlers means love and guidance,
***not** punishment.*

CHAPTER 12

Guiding Your Child Through Discipline

He went through the "No" stage pretty early—
from the time he was about a year old. It's rough. He
stands there and he says "No." Sometimes it makes
me pretty angry. We can't yell at him because he
really doesn't know what he's saying.

I'm surprised that we don't do much spanking.
Usually when we talk to him, he listens. We let him
play with a lot of things, but we watch him, and he
knows there is a limit.

Jarrod, 19 - Wade, 18 months (Valerie, 17)

I don't spank her. I just talk to her. I guess she can
tell by the tone of my voice. I got child abuse, and I'm
not going to touch my kid. I try to be a better parent
than my mom was.

*I take care of her and talk to her and let her know
by my mouth, not put my hands on her.*

*I know how much I didn't like being hit. I got put
out when I was 14. Right now I'm kind of violent at
times, and I feel she don't deserve something like that.*

Lorenzo, 17 - Aviantay, 2 years (Monique, 18)

What do you think of when you say "discipline"?
Punishment?

Discipline means to educate. It comes from the same
root as disciple, one who is taught. In this sense, your child
is your disciple.

It's your job to guide and teach your child to behave in
ways that will help him cope with the world he lives in.
Your teaching will help him have a more satisfying life,
both now as a child, and later as an adult.

You can discipline your child best in a child-safe place
with interesting things to explore and to use for play. The
most important part of discipline is making it *easy* for
children to behave correctly.

She Wants to Please You

*She's not two yet, and already she likes to please
us. When I'm stern with her, and I'm pretty big, she
listens. Whether or not she does what I say, she knows
something is wrong.*

*Two thoughts on this—I try not to overdo it be-
cause if you do, it loses its effect. The other thing is
that for the most part we're real nice to her, and she
likes us and she likes being with us. When I say
something stern, it matters to her.*

John, 21 - Mandi, 22 months (Danielle, 20)

Most of the time discipline is not a difficult task. Your
child by nature wants to please you. Usually she will try to
behave the way she thinks you expect her to behave.

Her natural curiosity and her drive to explore will cause problems at times. All children need some help to control or limit undesirable behavior. A caring relationship built on love and trust makes it easier for your child to accept limits on behavior.

Sharing Childrearing Beliefs

You and your partner need to share with each other your ideas on childrearing, especially in regard to discipline. Most parents have strong feelings about how a child should be handled.

If one parent has been brought up by parents who spanked a lot and the other wasn't, it may be hard for them to agree on discipline methods for their child.

It's important that everyone who interacts with your child agree as much as possible on discipline (learning) techniques.

Setting Limits

You'll have to set some limits. A child who always does whatever he feels like doing whenever he wants to do it is likely to cause problems for himself and others. Since limits cut back on his freedom to explore and learn, however, set as few as possible.

Once you've set a limit, stick with it. Being consistent is extremely important. Your limits define safe play areas and play things. Your limits provide a sense of security because he knows what he can do. He knows that someone is watching and caring.

He will learn about limits through discipline. Note, the word is discipline, not punishment. Punishment should not be a part of disciplining babies and toddlers.

She Learns by Exploring

At first, you'll need most of the discipline yourself. It is you who must stop the wrong behavior.

If she puts something dangerous or dirty in her mouth, it's up to you to take it out. Objects not to be touched must be out of her reach. You need to move her away from unsafe areas, or you need to set up barriers.

Alexis was beginning to get into stuff, and she'd make me mad. I'd keep telling her, "Don't do this, don't do that." I would yell at her a lot, but I'm trying not to yell so much now.

I need to put stuff up where she can't reach it. If I don't do that, I have to watch her a lot, because otherwise she'd crawl away. Work! Work! Work!

Dennis, 17 - Alexis, 6 months (Tara, 20)

Once she starts creeping or crawling, you will have a problem if your home is not child-proofed. She wants and *needs* to explore. That's how she learns.

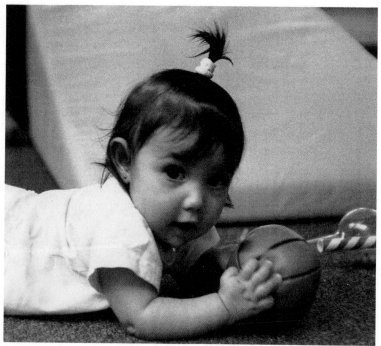

Her home is child-proofed—she can explore to her heart's content.

Making It Easy to Behave

Babies don't understand what they should or should not do. They simply must explore because that's where they are in their development.

Slapping his hands when he reaches for things isn't likely to change his behavior. It *can* damage his trust in you and make future discipline more difficult.

Make it easy for him to behave. If you don't want him to touch something, put it away!

When I left (for prison), Britney and Jakela were eight months old. They were starting to crawl, picking up different kinds of things.

They were pulling the telephone cord down, but we fixed that. My mother-in-law had two kinds of phones. We put the cordless phone downstairs and the cord phone upstairs so they couldn't get to it.

Alton, 17 - Britney and Jakela, 1 year (Sharrell, 19)

If he wants something he can't have, and it can't be put out of reach, you must take responsibility for keeping him away from it.

We're going to keep stuff off the tables so we won't have to say "No" all the time. Julie's mom has a coffee table with little coasters, flowers, stuff like that. We're talking to her about moving all that stuff away from the living room and the kitchen. She's willing.

Jason, 18 - Josh, 3 months (Julie, 17)

If you're unwilling or unable to child-proof your home, you must be willing and able to spend an enormous amount of time helping your child cope with his surroundings.

Eventually, of course, your child will learn that some things are his and some are not. Some things can be played with and others can't. This may not happen until he's nearly three or even older.

Shaken Infant Syndrome

Sometimes a parent shakes an infant or child who is misbehaving. This is a physically dangerous thing to do.

An infant's neck is quite weak. At first she can't even hold up her head. The head of an infant or even a child is large and heavy compared to the rest of her body. If she is shaken, her head will bounce back and forth between her back and her chest. She's not yet able to stiffen her neck muscles to protect it.

At this young age, her brain is smaller than the skull. This allows room for the rapid growth of the brain. Therefore, if her head is shaken, the brain will be tossed around within her skull. Her brain may become bruised and swollen. The shaking may cause some bleeding and blood clots as well. It can result in permanent brain damage or even death.

While many children will appear to survive a shaking without any handicap at all, they may not be as intelligent as they otherwise would have been. Problems with vision or learning may also appear later.

Even throwing a baby up in the air in play is not safe for these same reasons.

Toddlers and Discipline

Elena has always been a good baby, but she has her moments. Lately she's going through the Terrible Two stage where she wants to do only what she wants to do. Now she tells us "No." I try not to yell at her, and I don't want to hit her.

She'll go after something on the furniture, and we tell her not to get it. We tell her "No," and she looks at us, then takes it. We take it from her, and she'll take it again, then throw the stuff.

Carlos, 19 - Elena, 23 months (Monica, 18)

When this happens to you, don't yell. Get up and walk across the room. Tell your child what he should do as you move him away from what he can't have. If you yell your directions from a distance, he probably won't understand them. Even if he does, he's likely to ignore you.

He has little understanding of "right" or "wrong," or what could happen as the result of his actions. He has no idea that the delicate vase he just grabbed could slip out of his hands and break until it has done just that. Most toddlers are "good" if they happen to feel like doing what they should do and not doing what they should not.

Support his desire for independence by getting rid of any limits you don't really need. Limits that are needed, such as staying out of the street, *must* be firmly and consistently maintained.

Being Yelled At Hurts Him

You know how parents yell and say you can't do this and you can't do that? I don't want to yell or hit my son because I don't think that teaches you any-thing. When I was little, I got hit. It didn't teach me nothing. If you get hit all the time, pretty soon it don't hurt no more.

If he does real bad, I don't blow my top. I think about it first, then talk about it with him, and tell him why he shouldn't do this. When he's a baby, there's no way he should be punished.

Jimmy, 17 - Roman, 1 year (Rosalva, 19)

No one should ever discipline a child in anger. Too often in anger, people use tactics they don't want their child to copy. They're rude. They yell, they use bad language, and they make horrible threats.

Yelling is verbal abuse. It scares a child. It's hard on his self-esteem. Poor self-esteem is a nasty stumbling block not

only to good behavior, but to learning as well. If he feels he
isn't a good person, he won't act like one. That's not what
you want for your child.

We are our children's models. If we want our children to
respect other people, we have to show respect for them.
Yelling at him isn't showing respect.

Must Children Be Hit, Slapped, or Spanked?

Should children be slapped or spanked? Some people
say, "Yes," but more and more people are saying "No."
Usually they say "No" because they have discovered that
spanking doesn't work very well.

> *I don't believe in hitting. I ain't going to hit my*
> *son. I was hit,*
> *I hate to see people hurt, in pain, and I don't want*
> *to see Jaysay cry. I don't want him to go through*
> *what I went through. I been in homes, I had a real*
> *bad coming up, but I don't want him to go through*
> *all that.*
>
> Darrance, 17 - Jaysay, 1 year (Victoria, 17)

Hitting a child won't make her be obedient. There's no
way you can force her to eat her dinner or to urinate in the
toilet, for example.

Spanking or slapping a child is not a good idea for many
reasons. The baby or toddler will seldom understand why
you, someone he trusts, hit him to make him cry.

Even if he realizes that he displeased you, he now knows
that hurting people is all right, especially if you're bigger
and stronger. It must be—daddy or mother hit him. It's all
right to be a bully!

> *Spanking is not teaching them to stop. Hitting on*
> *them just makes them mad, and they do it again. But*
> *teaching, you show them they're not supposed to mess*
> *with it. As they grow older, they'll know that's wrong.*

> *When my family spanked me, I knew what I did was*
> *wrong—but it made me angrier and angrier, and I'd*
> *keep on doing it. I'd rob and everything, and they*
> *kept locking me up. Now that I have kids, I know*
> *there's no use treating them as I was treated.*
>
> Alton

Punishment Interferes with Learning

Punishment tries to control behavior by force, using pain and loss for effectiveness. It can interfere with learning because none of us learns as well when we're afraid. Punishment too often gives a child a feeling of failure.

> *You're closer to the one that doesn't spank you. I*
> *did what my dad said because he never hit me. Hitting*
> *isn't going to help anyway because you get hit and*
> *it's over. It don't make any difference.*
>
> Wayne, 17 - Ricky, 6 months (Charlene, 16)

Harsh punishment is emotionally scarring. While some children seek revenge, others become guilty and humiliated victims, people afraid to do anything for fear of failure. They don't learn to think for themselves.

Blind obedience is not the goal of discipline. Blind obedience will cause a child to be a follower who will do what other people tell her to do without judging whether it's right or wrong.

Child Abuse Happens

Another reason not to use hitting as punishment is the real danger of getting out of control. Physical child abuse is a tragic reality for many families in the United States. More than a million children are abused each year, and about 2,000 die from child abuse.

If a parent decides that hitting is a good method of punishment, that parent may be more likely to hit too hard than would the parent who doesn't believe in hitting in the first place. Parents who were spanked a lot or physically abused as children are more likely to abuse their children.

Males tend to be more aggressive, and around children you need to deal with this. Children don't need this.

How do you deal with the frustrations and angers of parenting? Take time out. If you need a break, find someone else to hold your child for a little while. Let things simmer down a bit, and avoid thinking it's a power struggle.

It's not a power struggle with the child. He's just exploring his world, testing his boundaries, learning what he can get away with. He doesn't do this to anger or upset you.

Greg, 17 - Liana, 1 year (Nicole, 17)

Helping Your Toddler Behave

You can and should limit your toddler's behavior with necessary restrictions. You can and should stop his activities when necessary either by removing him from the scene or helping him do what he must do. It is part of your job as his parent.

Many parents resort to an occasional swat on a diapered bottom. Their child survives nicely, but the fact remains— that swat probably didn't accomplish much. A child who is spanked is actually less likely to obey his parents in the future.

You can find discipline strategies that work without yelling, slapping, or hitting. Also take time to appreciate this delightful little person who is your child. Respect his need to explore and learn. Think about how you can help him succeed in his drive toward discovery. Then *both you and your child will win.*

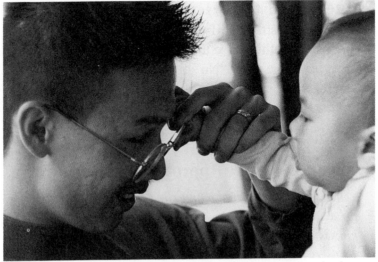

Glasses are to be explored. It's dad's job not to get them broken.

Discipline Strategies

Strategy 1. Use "No" Sparingly

"No" is an important word in discipline, but don't use it too often. Your goal when you say "No" is to get your child to react, to stop what he's doing. If he hears "No" every two minutes all day long, he's not going to respond.

> *We're just getting into discipline right now, and it's difficult. Liana's really getting a mind of her own. We try to use the word "No" as little as possible because otherwise it won't be effective.*
>
> *We've taught her words like "hot," and she understands. We use distraction as much as possible. The "No" only works to an extent, and if you overdo it, you end up becoming frustrated.*
>
> Greg

If he hears "No" only a few times a day, and he hears a different I-mean-it tone of voice, he will learn to react and obey. That's what you want.

Strategy 2. Distract Her

When you distract her from an unwanted activity by giving her something else to play with, you can often do so without using the word "No" at all.

"Here's your ball. Can you roll it to me?" works much better than saying to a nine-month-old baby, "No, don't do that." You're telling her what she *should* do instead.

Strategy 3. Positive Approach

It really bothers me when she says "No" and won't do what I tell her to do—especially when I know she knows exactly what I want. She won't look at me—she just sits there and won't do what I say.

John

Stoop down and get eye contact before you tell her what you want her to do. Then she'll be more likely to listen to you and understand what you're saying. She's getting a lot of information through your body language and facial expressions.

When you talk to her, give her positive rather than negative commands. Tell her what she should do rather than what she should not. Instead of saying, "Don't touch the vase," try "The vase needs to stay on the table." Instead of "Stop pulling the cat's tail," try "Let's pet the kitty gently."

Strategy 4. Give Him A Choice

Give him a choice whenever you can. "It's time for your bath. Do you want it in the tub or in the shower?" may get his cooperation faster than ordering, "Take your bath now." "Do you want lunch outside or in your high chair?" may make him more willing to leave his morning play than a command, "Come to lunch right now."

When you give him a choice, you're giving him a sense of control over his environment and a feeling of competence. This means he's less likely to defy you.

Keep the choices simple. Even then, he may have a difficult time sticking to his choice. For instance, if you ask him if he'd like apple juice or milk for his snack time, he may select the milk. Then he may become very upset if he can't have juice instead. Let him change his mind. That's all right.

Be sure the choices you give him are real. Don't ask him "Do you want to go to bed now?" if you've already decided he must go. Point to the clock and say "It's time to go to bed now. Which bedtime story would you like me to read?"

Strategy 5. Reinforce Behaviors You Like

Reinforcing good behavior is an important part of discipline. If, when your child is playing quietly, you ignore him, his behavior is not being reinforced. Instead, join him in his play or talk about what he's doing. For instance, tell him, "I like the way you stacked those blocks." Or sit quietly and watch him play.

> *Mandy's thrown only a couple of tantrums so far. We give her a lot of praise when she's a good girl. That's a lot of the time, and we try to reinforce that.*
>
> *We're fairly consistent. She really wants to be a good girl. I think a lot of that is attention. When you give them a lot of attention, they don't have to misbehave.*
>
> John

Toddlers need a lot of attention. Positive attention from significant persons makes learning more meaningful and important. Praise works so much better than punishment.

If he's getting your attention and companionship when he's behaving the way you want him to behave, he'll probably continue doing those things that draw the attention he craves. If he seems to get attention mostly through being naughty, he'll probably act naughty more often.

Strategy 6. Warning Before Activity Change

Many young children have a hard time changing activities. They become quite involved with what they're doing, and it's hard for them to stop.

Tell her a few minutes ahead of time when you want her to change her activity. Then she knows her play is about to be interrupted, and she can begin to think about what will happen next.

This will help her learn to anticipate and plan ahead. It will make the transition from one activity to the next much easier for both of you.

Strategy 7. Provide a Reward

A reward for a particular behavior should occur as a natural result of that behavior. For instance, tell her if she helps you pick up the toys, you'll have time to read her a story. If she cooperates in the supermarket, you'll stop at the park on the way home.

Many times the best reward is telling her that she did a good job and that you're proud of her. This is much more significant than saying she's a good girl. By recognizing her ability to do the task and to do it well, you help her feel competent. She'll feel able to learn even more.

Strategy 8. Time-Out May Help

Some people use time-out as a discipline technique. If the child is misbehaving, he is told to sit in a chair for a specified time. Usually a timer is used, and the parent says, "You may get down when the timer dings."

If you use time-out with a toddler, the time should be very short, perhaps a minute for each year of his age. Better yet, use time-out, but don't suggest that it's meant as a punishment.

When your toddler fusses, cries, or "acts out" and misbehaves, he's expressing distress. Hitting, biting, throwing toys or other objects may be an indication that the child has lost control of his behavior and may need help to regain it. Time-out might be that help.

Time-out need not be spent without any activity. It is not necessary or even desirable to set him on a chair in the corner. It can be time spent resting, or with a quiet activity away from noise and excitement or other stimulation. Your goal is not to punish your child, but to help and support him so he can get back in control.

Perhaps as he gets older, he will recognize his own need for rest and relaxation. This is more likely to happen if time-out has been a positive experience for him, and it has not been used to punish or embarrass him.

Strategies Instead of Punishment

You'll think of many other strategies that will work with your child. Using discipline strategies to help her behave appropriately makes childrearing much more effective than using punishment to force her to obey. With your discipline strategies, you not only help her learn self-control, you support her self-confidence. You give her self-respect.

Discipline begins with your relationship with your child. If you have a good relationship, she wants to please you just as you want to please her. You want to do things to make her feel good. She wants to do things to make you feel good.

Most important, good discipline demands an unending supply of love.

"You need time together to nurture and build a relationship." (Greg)

CHAPTER **13**

The Partnership Challenge

Parenting is a difficult thing. It takes its toll on both parents. Mothers need to understand that it's very difficult for fathers, and the fathers need to understand that the mothers need a break.

At least once a month they need to go out separately with their friends. You also need to make time throughout the month for you two to do something together. You need time to nurture and build a relationship.

Greg, 17 - Liana, 1 year (Nicole, 17)

The relationship between a teen father and his child's mother may range from marriage to no relationship at all. How you parent your child depends somewhat on your relationship with his mother. You can be a "good" parent whether or not you and his mother are friends, but it's harder if you're not.

Only one in three teenage mothers is married when her child is born. By the time the child is 3, a high percentage of these marriages have ended. By this time, many teenage parents are with different partners.

Making good decisions concerning partners is perhaps one of the hardest issues faced by teenage parents. There is likely to be even more heartbreak in a failed relationship when there is a child involved.

Is Marriage the Answer?

Are you thinking about marriage? Or maybe you're already married.

Thirty years ago, marriage was often the "answer" to too-early pregnancy. A pregnant teen's father might demand that his daughter and her boyfriend get married.

Some couples had many years of happiness together. For many other couples, it didn't work. Teenagers change rapidly as they grow older.

A boy and girl who marry at 16 may no longer share the same interests at 20. They may be two very different people. A couple married at 16 is four times more likely to separate than is the couple who marries after 22.

If there is something wrong with the relationship now, marriage won't fix it.

Making the Marriage Decision

If you and your partner are considering marriage, you may want to discuss such things as:

• Do you have a place to live? For most couples, it's harder to develop a good relationship while you're living with other people.

- Do you both want to spend *all* the rest of your life together?
- Are you working and earning enough to support your family? Or will you and your partner both work and share in the care of your child?
- Do you agree on such important questions as:
  - When will you have your next child?
  - Will either or both of you continue going to school?
  - Who is expected to have a job? Husband? Wife? Both?
  - Who will take primary responsibility for the care of your child?

You can think of a lot of other things you need to discuss thoroughly before you decide to spend the rest of your lives together.

The two of you might like to read *Teenage Marriage: Coping with Reality* (Morning Glory Press) together. You'll find a lot of suggestions for making a partnership work, whether you're married or simply living with your partner.

Communicating with Your Partner

At the back of *Teenage Marriage* is a "Score Card" for teenage marriage decisions. You'll also find a fairly long questionnaire concerning attitudes toward marriage and living together. You and your partner might each like to take this "test," then compare your answers. It might help you see more clearly the areas in which you agree and those in which you disagree.

Completing the questionnaire together is also an excellent way to help you start talking about some important issues. Too often, partners don't communicate well about money, children, families, home preferences, career goals, and other vitally important topics.

Stresses of Living Together

Erica thought about abortion, but decided to continue the pregnancy. A week or two later we decided to get married.

She moved in here with me and my parents until Kevin was born. Living with each other is tough. When we were that young we really didn't know each other as good as we thought—it was almost our first relationship.

It's hard living with your parents, too. I'd have to say, "Don't start with the marriage right away. You don't need to get married."

We lived here the whole time. We went through Lamaze. The pregnancy was hard. I finally got a job, and I worked after school every day plus weekends and holidays.

I was very tired all the time. Erica thought when we got married we'd spend more time together. Because of me working, we actually had less time. She'd say, because she was young, "Don't go to work today," but I had to.

When I'd come home, she'd want to play. I'd say, "I'm really tired right now," and she thought I was rejecting her.

Zach, 19 - Kevin, 20 months (Erica, 16)

If you're living together, your relationship will have its ups and downs, just as an older couple would experience.

You may have added stress because of lack of money and dependence on your families. One or both of you may still be in school. Juggling school, parenting, and possibly a job can get crazy.

Having a good relationship in the middle of all this stress is difficult. Good relationships take time and effort in addition to love, just as good parenting takes time and effort in addition to love. Finding time for both your partner and your child may seem almost impossible.

> *Friday night we go to the movies. I feel it's very important that a couple spend time with each other. You need the time away, and it helps keep your relationship going. Having a child is such a responsibility, it gets to be overwhelming at times.*
>
> Dennis, 17 - Alexis, 6 months (Tara, 20)

Making time for each other may be difficult, but it's important to your relationship.

Sometimes people talk about a good relationship being a 50-50 situation—each partner has equal rights and responsibilities. A better percentage is probably 60-60 — each partner goes *more* than half way to please the other. At the same time, each of you needs to guard his/her own self-esteem. You do this even as you do *more* that your share in maintaining a loving and caring relationship.

Being honest and trusting with each other is essential.

Three-Generation Living

If you and your partner live with your parents or hers, this may add stress to your relationship.

> *Her parents are a lot different than mine. Her mom always had to add her two cents in on everything we did. She was practically telling us how to raise Deziree. It was rough.*
>
> *We tried to make it work. We stayed out of the house as much as possible. We'd take Deziree to the park or to a friend's house.*
>
> *Generally we just took it. We figured they're giving us this place to stay, and we have to take it until we can get our own place. We've lived here for a year.*
>
> *Now we finally have enough money to move into our own apartment.*
>
> Purnell, 18 - Deziree, 18 months (April, 20)

Being somebody's son and following the rules of the house can be frustrating when you're also someone's dad, and you've taken on adult responsibilities. You'll feel less stress if you accept your current situation and make it work as well as possible—while you work hard toward becoming self-sufficient and able to support your family.

People Are Not for Hitting

Some teenage (and older) men resort to hitting their partner when they're frustrated. Sometimes the woman beats on the man, but it's the woman who is most likely to be hurt. And no one wins an argument by using force or physical strength. If you resort to violence, she won't agree with you because you're right, but because you're physically stronger.

Beating someone doesn't solve problems, and it doesn't help a relationship. It makes things worse.

A man who hits a woman, he must not really be a man. There are ways to handle a situation without physical contact. That's wrong. I never hit my lady friend. We get into arguments, but when I get angry, I walk away. It doesn't take violence.

Jamal, 16 - Valizette, 16 months (Shawnteé, 17)

Learn to argue without hitting on each other. There are better ways to solve problems than hitting:

When I get frustrated, I leave. I go running, do something like that. That way I don't take it out on my girlfriend or my kid.

Tony, 16 - Felipe, 16 months (Alicia, 17)

Talk to each other when you have problems. If you have a problem and you leave it in, it doesn't help. I still do that to some extent, but not much.

When you're mad at someone else, don't take it out on your partner.

And take it one day at a time.

Dennis

If you know someone who is being abused, you might want to suggest *Breaking Free from Partner Abuse* (1993: Morning Glory Press). This book offers help for women in abusive relationships. It's underlying theme is, "You don't deserve this."

When Parents Separate

The relationship with your partner may be more complicated because you're a parent. If it's a poor relationship, you may, because of your child, not feel free to leave.

If you do split, you *can* continue parenting your child.

Our relationship is not going to work. There are too many bad parts about it.

That crushes my heart, not having the kids. I'm used to putting them to bed, kissing them in the morning before I go to work. I'll still get to see them.

I know the kids are going to ask why I left mom. I hope she'll explain why. I'd never say anything bad about their mother. When my mom and dad divorced, they talked bad about each other, and I didn't know what to think. I was confused.

Sometimes I'm scared that my children won't really know me because they won't see me every day, only on weekends.

Luis, 20 - Benito, 8 months; Karina, 3 (Myndee, 21)

When the mother and father split up, the mother is more likely to have the day-to-day responsibility of child rearing. When this happens, dad needs to make an effort regularly to spend as much time as possible with his child.

Some fathers get custody when the couple splits. Zach and Erica were married a year, then divorced. Zach continues to live with his parents and care for his child. Erica visits Kevin regularly:

We'd get in fights, and Erica would leave. She'd take a walk or go over to her mom's. I'd get all scared and go look for her.

Finally Erica and Kevin moved back to her mom. They wanted me to pay a baby-sitter so she could start school, but I wasn't making enough money. Then one night I was at a friend's, and I guess Erica was all fed up. She brought Kevin over here and left.

The next day I told her we'd keep Kevin. She said I'd never let her see him, and I said she could see him whenever she wanted. Kevin has stayed here since then. We've been divorced for several months. Mom helps me, but I've taken most of the responsibility.

Zach

Would you like to have custody of your child? If you aren't with your baby's mom, and you're concerned that she is not being responsible, talk with someone about the possibility of getting custody. Perhaps your mom, an aunt, or other responsible adult could help you consider your options.

If You Must Be Away

Some couples who are "together" are separated for months or even years. He or she may be in jail. He or she may be in the armed forces. Or there could be other reasons for their separation.

If you're an absent parent, you know how much effort and determination it takes to remain close to your partner and your child. If a parenting class is available, taking it might help you understand better the stages through which your child is going. You'd have an idea of the behavior to expect when you return home.

Do the best you can to keep track of what's going on. Even though you're away, stay in with your child as much as you can. Get information about how he's doing developmentally, changes in his attitude. How does he act around this person, then around someone else? Keep learning as much as you can. Even though you're away, you can still know how fast he's growing, how he's progressing, the funny things he does.

Marc, 16 - Koary, 14 months (Melinda, 18)

Letters, photographs, and phone calls are extremely important during this time. See page 131.

Jamal shared his frustration of being locked up and losing touch with his baby and the baby's mother:

Back when we were together, I was around all the time. I was still going places with my friends, but if

*she needed me, I wouldn't go out. I was with the baby
a lot.*

*Then I started getting in more trouble in the
streets. I was always getting locked up, and finally I
was sent away. She was sending me pictures, then all
of a sudden I came home, and it was a whole lot
different.*

*I came over to see the baby, and we sort of stared
at each other. I don't know what happened. I got out
and everything changed. A lot of arguments came
between us. We stopped talking to each other, and she
don't want me around the baby.*

*I tried to talk to her, but every time I talk, she have
an attitude. Then I get angry, and I say I'm through
with it. Then I think about my baby, and I talk to her
again, but she don't want to see me.*

*I think I should help take care of the baby even
though we're apart. It's both our responsibilities.*

*Even if she doesn't want to be with me, that's still
my responsibility. We don't have to talk. I made that
child. He's part of me.*

Jamal

If Shawnteé won't let him see his child, Jamal needs to
talk to a lawyer to learn about his rights, as discussed in
Chapter 15. In most states, unless the court rules otherwise,
the father has a right to see his child.

It's better, of course, to be with your child because both
you and the child's mother know this is best for your child.
Jamal's best chance of having a satisfying relationship with
Valizette might be to talk out his differences with
Shawnteé. They don't need to have a close relationship
even if they are both going to parent this child. However,
they need to be willing to talk to each other and to be civil
to each other as they parent their child.

Building Trust

Lourdes brings Ricardo over once a week, and they stay four or five hours. Sometimes she leaves with the baby, but comes back later the same day.

She thinks I'm going to take Ricardo somewhere, and she won't see him. I tell her to trust me and take my word for it. I tell her I never took anything away from her that she loved, and I'm certainly not going to do it now.

Most of the time Ricardo sleeps. I change his diaper when he wakes up. We play around when he's awake. When I'm holding Ricardo, Lourdes has to be right next to me because she thinks I'm going to do something. She acts like she thinks I'm going to run.

Angel, 18 - Ricardo, 3 months (Lourdes, 19)

If Angel continues welcoming his child and Lourdes, Lourdes may start trusting him with Ricardo. She may realize how much he loves his son and, even more important, how Ricardo enjoys his time with his dad.

Perhaps Angel can work toward regular and longer visits with his son. If he truly wants to be an influence in Ricardo's life, he needs to do all he can to further their relationship.

There are no easy answers, but your concern for your child will help you work through your realities. Do the best you can wherever you are in your relationship with your child's mother. And remember—*your child needs you.*

*Some couples choose to delay their next pregnancy
so they can give this child the care she needs.*

CHAPTER 14

Another Baby — When?

*Another baby? Not very soon. We're pretty careful
with contraception because we don't want another
baby right away. That would be hard because we'd be
spending twice as much on diapers and everything
else. It would make everything harder.*

*It'll also be easier when Keegan is 3 or 4 years old
because he'll know more. He won't cry as much.
We've agreed to wait.*

Randy, 17 - Keegan, 2 months (Whitney, 15)

Planning Your Family

Many teen mothers and fathers who have one child are
able to continue their education and work toward their
goals. If they have a second child before they have finished
school, the difficulties multiply. Having more than one

child limits one's independence drastically.

Many teen couples get pregnant again. Half of all teen mothers have another baby within two years.

Couples need to think and talk about future family plans. How soon do you want another child? Many young mothers and fathers, whether married or not, don't want another baby right away. There are many reasons for waiting:

- You want to give your first child the care he needs. Toddlers need a great deal of attention.

- Outside care for one child is hard to find. Finding someone to care for two children is even harder.

- More babies cost more money. Do you have enough?

- She's less likely to have a healthy baby if her next pregnancy happens too soon after the first one.

- Having too many children could hurt your relationship with your partner.

After I had the baby, Brian wanted to use two condoms in case one broke! We're really into it. I don't take the pill, but we always use the condom and foam.

Neither of us will do anything if we don't have protection. Either one of us will say, "Do you have a condom? Foam?"

Erin, 16 - Alex, 12 months (Brian, 20)

Babies do come by accident. If you don't want another child right away, birth control is essential. This could be simply not having intercourse, but most parents will want some other kind of contraceptive. If she's breast-feeding, don't count on it to keep her from getting pregnant. She can get pregnant even though she's breast-feeding.

Sexually active couples need to discuss their thinking concerning contraception. If this is difficult for you, remember that having another baby too soon would also be hard on your partner. Brad talked about this issue:

*I'd rather have three years between children. I
want my first son to have time for me to teach him.*

*How to talk about sex with your partner? First of
all, be alone. Ask her how she feels about using
protection. How many kids do you want to have? If
one or the other doesn't want to use protection, they
have to talk it through.*

Brad, 17 - Maria, 13 months (Carole, 16)

Some young women say their partners don't want them
to use birth control. One student told us her boyfriend
wouldn't "let" her use birth control. He thought if she did,
she might have sex with other guys.

A relationship with so little trust between the partners
must be in trouble.

Lots of Options

Do you and your partner want to delay her next pregnancy? Plan now how you'll do so. There are a wide
variety of contraceptives. Look at what's available. Then
decide which is best for you.

You and your partner don't need a prescription for
several contraceptives. You can buy these in almost any
drugstore. These include:

• condom (rubber)

• spermicidal jelly or foam

• cervical sponge

• suppositories

All of these kill sperm or keep them out of the uterus.

The condom helps prevent the spread of STDs (sexually
transmitted diseases).

STDs (Sexually Transmitted Diseases): Illness
spread through sexual intercourse.

The man needs to put the condom on carefully. He does this *before* his penis touches his partner's genitals.

He rolls the condom on his erect penis. He should leave one-half inch of space at the end of the condom. This will make it feel more comfortable. It will also be less likely to break.

Remember, if you use a condom and she uses foam, the two methods together are as successful at preventing conception as is the pill or the IUD. Both the condom and foam can be bought at a drugstore with no prescription from the doctor.

Your local health department may provide the condom, foam, and jelly at no charge.

Teen Fathers Comment on Condoms

One young man, when asked if the man should be responsible for birth control, replied, "No, it's the mother's responsibility. I don't like to use condoms. I'll rely on my partner."

Other young fathers quoted in this book reacted strongly and negatively to his statement:

Tony, 16: *I'd recommend he use condoms. That's true— condoms don't feel right, but it doesn't matter whether it feels right or not. You should still use them.*

Agie, 18: *If you don't like the way it feels, I guess you're taking a chance to get a disease or to get a baby. It takes everything to raise a baby. If he's going to get together like that, go ahead if you want a baby or a disease.*

Jamal, 16: *That's a person who wants to catch AIDS or other STDs. At first I thought that about condoms, but when I see something that will harm me, I try to stop it. And unprotected sex is very, very harmful.*

Luis, 20: *That's stupid, not using a condom. You both*

should take precautions. You don't like the feel of the rubber, you can sit there and wait until you decide to use it.

Jarrod, 19: *Well, if he doesn't want to use condoms, I don't think he should be having sex.*

Before Valerie got pregnant, I didn't care for condoms, but it's something you learn to live with. It saves a lot of problems later down the road because now sometimes I sit and wonder where I'd be if I didn't have Wade. Then I sit there and think how would I live without him? If I would have known then what I know now, though, it would probably be different.

Don't count on withdrawal (pullout) to prevent pregnancy. (This means the man takes his penis out of the woman's body before he ejaculates.) Some people think no sperm will reach the egg if he comes outside her body. *This is not true.* Sperm leave the penis *before* ejaculation.

Withdrawal is *not* a reliable method of birth control. As a school nurse commented, "I've seen lots of cute little pullout babies!"

Birth Control Pill

Birth control pills for women are widely available from doctors and clinics. Insurance or Medicaid may pay for the pill.

She doesn't have to take the pill right before having sex. That's an advantage. She does have to take one *every* day.

Birth control pill

It's easy to forget it. Tyson reminds me. We never talked about birth control before I got pregnant. I didn't think it would happen to me—but it did.

Frederica, 16 - Jesse, 5 months (Tyson, 19)

Is she breast-feeding the baby? Taking the pill might cut back on her supply of milk. If she's breast-feeding, she should talk to her doctor. It might be best to choose another contraceptive until she weans baby to bottle or cup. Some pills, however, don't affect the making of breast milk.

Note: The pill will *not* prevent pregnancy the first month she takes it. If you have sex during that time, use another contraceptive.

The pill will *not* protect either of you from STDs including AIDS.

Spermicides

Spermicide: Product that kills sperm.

The woman can use foam or jelly (spermicide) right before she has sex. She puts it in her vagina with a special little tool. Used alone, foam or jelly is not a reliable method of preventing pregnancy.

Foam or jelly work best when the man uses a condom.

IUD—Another Method for Women

The IUD (Intrauterine Device) for women is a plastic device about an inch long. It comes in various shapes.

The doctor places the IUD in the woman's uterus. Once there, it stays in for several years.

The IUD is for women who have had a child. A woman using it should be having sex with only one man. With several partners, she would be more likely to get an infection from the IUD.

IUD

Contraceptive Implant

The newest family planning device is the implant. It is a low dose of birth control medicine in a capsule. The doctor puts the capsule under the skin of the woman's upper arm. It doesn't show.

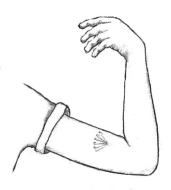

Contraceptive implant

Once there, it slowly releases the pregnancy-preventing medicine. This continues for at least one year. Some may prevent pregnancy for five years. Her insurance may cover the cost of the implant.

Neither the IUD nor the implant prevents the spread of STDs including AIDS. Only condoms can do that.

STD Concerns

Sexually active people should be concerned about STDs. Some STDs are merely annoying, such as a yeast infection.

Others have serious and long-lasting effects. They need immediate treatment. AIDS is an STD that causes death.

Some STDs have obvious symptoms such as large sores on the skin. Others might not show anything on the outside at all. You can't be sure by looking at someone whether or not she has a disease.

> *Because of the diseases today, men should still wear condoms. They're a pain in a way, but it's either do you want to live or die any more.*
> Paul, 19 - Katherine, 4 months (Kyla, 15)

The best way not to get an STD is not to have sex. Next best is for the man to use a condom. It's safer if the woman uses a spermicidal jelly while the man uses a condom.

If you or your partner ever have any of these symptoms, see your doctor or go to a clinic:

- Painful urination (both men and women)
- Unusual discharge from the penis or vagina
- Sore or itching genitals
- Lumps or growths around genital areas
- Rashes or blisters on the genital area
- Sores on the penis, on the vulva, or in the vagina

Remember: Most STDs can be treated. Early treatment prevents serious lifelong effects. Medicaid and private insurance pay for this care. Public health departments provide free or very low cost treatment for STDs.

AIDS—An Incurable STD

AIDS cannot be treated successfully. AIDS stands for Acquired Immune Deficiency Syndrome.

The AIDS virus makes the body unable to fight diseases. A person with AIDS could die from any disease. Most often, cancer or pneumonia is the cause of death.

There are no early symptoms of AIDS. There is no cure. People who have AIDS are treated for their symptoms. However, they will not be cured.

In the past, some people got AIDS through blood transfusions. This is almost impossible today. Blood for transfusions is now thoroughly tested for the AIDS virus.

Today people get AIDS by:
- Having sex with an infected person
- Sharing needles with infected people
- Having sex with someone who shares needles with IV drug users
- Being infected before or during birth by mother

Caring for Yourself and Your Family

The more partners you have, the more likely you are to get an STD.

Things you can do to avoid STDs:

- Think about other ways to have a loving
  relationship.
- Protect both of you by using a condom during
  intercourse.
- Discuss protection from pregnancy *before* you begin
  sexual intercourse.
- Consider the risks of both pregnancy and STDs for
  you and your partner.

Planning for Your Next Child

Have your next child when you and your partner are
ready—

• physically   • emotionally   • financially

This will be better for your present child and for your
future family.

*She's on the pill and I use a condom. We don't
push our luck—it's too easy to slip up.*

*I think all my friends used to think they couldn't get
a girl pregnant, and now they realize they have to be
extra careful. Two of my friends have been together
for a year, and they haven't slept together yet because
we keep telling them it's not that important.*

*Heather was on the pill when she got pregnant, but
she wasn't very responsible about taking it. Now
every night I make sure she takes her pill before we
go to bed. We don't want another baby right now.*

Jacob, 17 - Melanie, 13 months (Heather, 17)

If you and your partner don't want to be pregnant again,
plan *now* to prevent it:

- Choose not to have sex, *or*

- If you're having intercourse, use birth control—*always.*

It's up to you and your partner to make this happen. And
if your partner isn't interested, *it's up to you.*

Graduating from high school is a positive step toward a good future for yourself, your baby, and baby's mom.

CHAPTER 15

Your Future—
Your Child's Future

*I had a job, but I lost it because business got slow.
Once you lose that job, it's hard to find another one.*

*I was trying to make it in sports, a professional
athlete, but Amy busted that dream. I was thinking
about going into the Army, but I thought about being
that far away from them . . . yes, I'd be putting food
on the table, give them money, but a child needs her
father regardless.*

*A child needs a father with her. If the father is
working, he got to take time out from work and spend
time with his child.*

*I went back to school because I want to graduate. I
want to be a fireman, and I can do that with six
months of training.*

Jermaine, 18 - Amy, 12 months (Angela, 17)

Looking Ahead

What kind of future are you planning for you and for
your child? If you're with his mother, are you developing a
satisfying life together? Are you already an independent
family, or on your way to becoming independent?

Are you spending lots of time with your child—touching, loving, and playing with him? Do you help care for
him—feed him, change him, bath him? These are all part of
the "responsibility" thing. So is driving mom and baby to
doctor appointments. You just being there is important to
your child. Being a dad is far more than fathering a baby.

If you aren't with your child's mother, are you still
playing an important role in his life? Are you able to spend
time with him regularly? Even if you don't live with him,
you're an important part of his life.

Are you able to support your child? If you aren't to that
point, what are you doing now to get there? Are you still in
school? Are you learning job skills? It's essential that you
be able to support yourself and your child.

Your Responsibilities as a Father

*I see the babies with their moms and I wonder,
"How can you have a kid in this world and not want
it?" It's a part of you. I couldn't have my kid running
around without me.*

                    Jacob, 17 - Melanie, 13 months (Heather, 17)

As a teenager, it's hard to "take your responsibilities"
as a father, especially your financial responsibilities. If
you haven't finished high school, finding a good job isn't
easy. Even if you have graduated, it won't be easy. The
unemployment rate among teenage men is high.

If you're not working, people think you don't want to be
responsible. If you've left school, they write you off as

a typical teen father dropout. They think you will force your baby's mother to go on welfare.

Legally, you should provide for at least half of your child's support until she is 18. That's scary for a teenager with no job. Taking that responsibility at age 15—or even 18—may be impossible.

If you aren't yet 18, you may not be required to pay child support now. Laws vary from one state to another. However, many fathers, even with limited income, manage to provide some support for their child even as they continue their education and job training.

If you realize the cost of supporting a baby, you may feel like giving up. Many young fathers do. If they don't have money to pay for their baby's needs, they may give little or no help of any kind. Many others help as much as possible even as they continue their education and job training.

Establishing Paternity

If you aren't married to your child's mother, have you established paternity? It's important to do so for several reasons:

Identity: Your child needs to know who he is. There's a sense of belonging that comes from knowing both parents.

Benefits: Your child has a right to benefits from both parents. These may include Social Security, insurance benefits, inheritance rights, veterans' and other types of benefits. Unless you establish paternity, your child may not be able to claim these benefits through you.

Money: Both parents are required by law to support their child. A child who must rely on only one parent for financial support is likely not to have enough money for his needs.

Medical: Are there any health problems in your family? Your child needs to know.

If you aren't married to your child's mother, you establish legal paternity by affidavit, a legal paper that states you are the father of the child. Both you and your child's mother need to sign this affidavit. The actual procedure varies from state to state.

If you're the legal father, this gives you rights if the mother wants to place the child for adoption or if the authorities are trying to take the child away from the mother. You have *no* rights unless you have established legal paternity. If the state takes the child because the mother is on drugs, for example, you have no rights to your child if you haven't taken this step.

It's easier to establish paternity while you and the mother have a good relationship.

After she brought the baby home, her parents tried to keep me away from her. They would call the police. We weren't getting along, but now everything is working out okay.

If you're not married to your child's mother, it's important that you establish legal paternity.

*I went to a lawyer to learn about my rights. I also
wanted to go down and establish visitation rights.
Every man should know—you sign the birth certificate, but you still need to go to the courthouse and
she says under oath, "Yes, he's the father, I'm the
mother." If there's disagreements, you have to get a
blood test.*

*We still plan on getting married, but I want to
establish that I'm the father, and that I'll pay child
support.*

*Some women think it's not necessary, but I feel
every father should establish paternity. Then if the
woman ever says, "I don't want you," it's done.*

Paul, 19 - Katherine, 4 months (Kyla, 15)

Proving You're the Father

Is there any doubt that you're the father? You can find
out with nearly 100 percent accuracy through blood testing.
This is a genetic test that compares many different factors
in your blood with similar parts of the mother's and the
child's blood.

If your child's mother marries someone else, you will
still have rights and responsibilities toward your child.
You'll still need to pay child support. Most important, you
and your child will still have a right to know and to have a
relationship with each other. You should be able to have
visitation rights. Your child deserves both a mother and
a father.

*Ricardo is going to get hooked on to thinking that
Lourdes' boyfriend is his father. I tell Lourdes there's
going to be a time they'll have to tell Ricardo that's
not his real father. I want Ricardo to grow up
knowing I'm his real father.*

I thought about forgetting about the baby because I

have a lot of family problems, but I can't do that.
He's something I created. A father should be there for
his kid whether or not it was a mistake.

Angel, 18 - Ricardo, 3 months (Lourdes, 19)

It's best to establish paternity as early as possible. If you wait, things may change and you might not have a chance to assume responsibility for your child. She might grow up without knowing you and without the benefits that come from having both parents share in parental responsibilities.

You can help give your baby the best possible chance in life by getting paternity established as soon as possible after she's born.

If you and your baby's mother don't live together, who does your baby live with? While mom is more likely to have day-to-day custody, you may have as much right to custody as mom does. Or you and baby's mom might share custody.

Taking Financial Responsibility

Julio had a low-paying job and, like many young fathers, wondered how he could possibly support his family:

I was working a construction job, making just a little over minimum wage. I thought, "Here we are, bringing a child into the world, and I'm going to have to support the child." I told the construction crew I was going to be a dad, and I wanted some advice.

"Leave now," they told me.
And "Get an abortion."

I hung in there, and when Francene was born, we had benefits so the medical bills were paid. But so much else was on my mind. Will I be able to afford food? The bills? The responsibilities never end.

I was worried about being a father. How do you fill a father's shoes, someone who's supposed to have all the answers? How do you live up to a father's reputation?

Julio, 24 - Francene, 4; Alina, 3; Gloria, 1 (Joanne, 22)

Whether you're the father or the mother, you need to live up to a parenting "reputation," as Julio says. You'll never have all the answers—none of us do—but you'll need to be responsible for your child. Being responsible includes being financially responsible as well as providing the companionship, love, and emotional support your child needs from you.

Job Helps Self-Esteem

A job can make a big difference in the way you feel about yourself. When you think well of yourself, when you have good self-esteem, you're a better father than when you're unhappy with yourself.

Even if you're out of high school, you may need more job training. Check community college catalogs for job training facilities. Possibilities may include Regional Occupation Programs (ROP) and high school career centers.

Also check for programs in your community that are funded by JTPA (Job Training Partnership Act). Your local Department of Social Services office could probably provide information.

> *I'll graduate a year from now. Right now I'm taking an ROP class—auto mechanics. If I don't get a job, I'll go to special training. They will teach me everything about a car, and it's free to ROP students. You learn six hours a day for a year plus you work part-time. Then they help you get a job.*
>
> *I want always to be able to get a job, and auto mechanics will do that.*

Raul, 16 - Marijo, 10 months (Sandra, 17)

Money Versus Happiness

Money doesn't buy happiness, but the lack of "enough" money can certainly cause a great deal of unhappiness. As you plan your future, it's important that you plan how you'll earn enough money to support your child.

I was working for six months and that kept us off welfare. Then I got laid off. Roxanne was working, and she got laid off, too. She applied for welfare, but that barely covers our rent.

I had planned to go to college. I thought the baby was going to be small forever. Soon she'll be a year old, and I still have another year of high school.

I hope I can take her to the college childcare center while I get some training. I want to work with the phone company fixing the lines.

Damon, 16 - Samantha, 8 months (Roxanne, 15)

Even if the two parents are together and both are working, they may have heavy financial problems. Money

Babies are expensive — and wonderful.

seldom stretches as far as they'd like. The couple may not agree on how to spend the money they have:

> *Kyla doesn't understand that money isn't like water. You have to work for it. It's tough.*
>
> *She doesn't see the difference between needing something and wanting something. If we can't have what we want now, maybe we can in the future, but it takes time. This causes a lot of fights.*
>
> Paul

Perhaps you and your partner could use some help in money management. You could probably find a class on this topic at your adult school. This might help you get the most benefit possible from the money you earn.

When You Have Other Problems

> *I'm always in the house. I'm in the house because if I go somewhere, I might get in trouble. I used to always hang around my friends and do dumb stuff, and now I realize I've got someone to take care of. Breanna needs me while she's growing up, someone to play baseball with her, someone to look up to. I made her, I need to take care of her.*
>
> Hugo, 16 - Breanna, 9 months (Marcella, 18)

Of course not all problems come with dollar signs. Teen parents, like everyone else, have ups and downs in their lives.

You may already be in school, or you may have a job. You may be making plans for your future and for your child's future. If, however, your life is not going the way you want it to go, have you considered getting extra help? You don't have to handle everything by yourself.

If you're having more problems than you can handle by yourself, the first step is to accept the fact that you need help. Some people find it very hard to admit they aren't making it on their own.

You're probably already getting informal help. Families often are a good source of support. So are friends. In fact, other young parents can offer tremendous support simply because they're facing some of the same problems that are bothering you.

Is there a group at your school or in your community for teen fathers? If not, perhaps you could talk to a counselor, a teacher, or youth leader, and get such a group started.

Daric joined a group for teen fathers at his school. It helped:

> *A lot of times I feel like I can't make it any more. I need support, and I don't get it at home much.*
>
> *I get a lot of support in the group. It helps a lot knowing I'm not the only one in this situation. It makes me feel a lot better.*

> Daric, 16 - Kianna, 1 year (Kim, 18)

Finding Community Resources

You may need help beyond what your family and friends can give. Perhaps they can suggest community resources for you to contact. Inquire about resources from other people with whom you interact—the director of a child-care center, your minister, doctor, or teacher. Check with your YMCA, youth clinic, and other local youth resources.

Also look in your telephone book. Your county or state Mental Health Association and Psychology Department at your local college may recommend counseling services.

If you or your partner is receiving AFDC (welfare), ask to see a social worker when you need special help. Social workers often have far too heavy case loads, but some are able to provide extra help to their clients.

If you have a local community center, the social worker there may be able to tell you where to go for help with your problems. Your hospital social service department may be a good resource.

More than 300 agencies in the United States are connected with the Family Service Association of America. These agencies offer individual and family counseling at low cost, as well as a variety of other family services.

For the agency in your area, check your telephone directory under the following listings: Family Service Association, Council for Community Services, County Department of Health, Counseling Clinic, Mental Health Clinic, or United Way.

Don't Give Up

Generally you can get a list of hot lines from your telephone operator. Dial "411," then say, "I have this type of problem. Can you help me?"

You may find, as you call hot lines and other community services, that phone numbers you have been given are not helping you. Too often the number has been changed, your call is answered by a recording, or the person responding tells you that agency can't help you.

When this happens, don't give up. If a person answers your call but can't help, ask for referrals. Tell him/her you need help. You don't know where to call next. Explain how much you would appreciate any ideas s/he may give you.

Marriage and family counselors are usually listed in the telephone yellow pages. Your area may have a cost-free counseling agency, or the cost may be based on income. If you have very little income, you may not be charged a fee.

Independence and self-sufficiency are wonderful things—if they work. All of us need extra help at some time in our lives. If this is your time of special need, do whatever is necessary to get that help. Both you and your child will be glad you did.

You and your child deserve the best there is. If you get

your education and improve your vocational skills, *you* can
be in charge of your life.

Your Long-Range Goals

Long-range goals are important too. You may have long-
range plans for your child as Andy does:

> *I want Gus to grow good. I don't want him to be in
> the streets or nothing. I'm going to try to teach him
> what's right and what's wrong. I don't want him to
> grow up like I did or like my brothers.*
>
> Andy, 17 - Gus, five months (Yolanda, 15)

Andy's goal is fine, but the important thing is, what is he
doing now to work toward that goal? Does it mean moving
to a different neighborhood? Taking parenting classes?
Improving his relationship with his child's mother?

Whatever your situation is, look at your goals for your
child, then plan how to accomplish those goals.

Long-range goals are important for you, too. Where do
you want to be in five years? What do you want to be
doing? What kind of job will you have?

The problem with long-range goals, however, is that
sometimes they may seem too easy. You may say, "In five
years, I'll have a college degree and a well-paying job.
We'll be married, have another baby, and a house."

That's a long-range goal, and if this is what you want, by
all means continue planning and working toward it.

Most important, what are you doing this year, *this month*
to work toward the life you want for yourself and your
child? What must you do in order to continue your education? What steps can you take *now* to begin or continue
your job skills training?

*What are you doing today to make a satisfying future for
yourself and your child?*

Appendix

About the Author

Jeanne Warren Lindsay has worked with hundreds of pregnant and parenting teenagers. She developed the Teen Mother Program

at Tracy High School, Cerritos, California, in 1972, and continues as a consultant in the program. She is the author of 14 other books dealing with adolescent pregnancy and parenting. Her *Teens Parenting* four-book series is widely used with pregnant and parenting teens.

Jeanne has graduate degrees in Anthropology and Home Economics. She and Bob have five children and five grandchildren.

About the Photographer

David Crawford, M.A., has been a teacher and photographer of family life for 25 years. He has worked with thousands of pregnant

and parenting teens as the co-director of the Program for Pregnant and Parenting Students, Daylor High School, Elk Grove Unified School District, Sacramento, California. David uses photography as a teaching aid, blending the art of photography with education and enhancement of students' self-esteem.

David and Peggy have a son, Alton, 23. They have also co-parented Terrica, daughter of one of David's former students.

Bibliography

The following books and pamphlets are especially for or about teenage fathers, or they provide parenting and other information of interest to young fathers. If you can't find a specific book or other resource in your bookstore, you can usually order it directly from the publisher. Enclose $2.50 for shipping in addition to the price of the book. Prices, when given, are from the 1992-1993 edition of *Books in Print.*

Books about teen fathers and teen father programs, but written for professionals, are listed in the Teacher's Guide for *Teen Dads.*

"Advice from Teens on Buying . . . Condoms." 1988. Folded leaflet, 25¢ each, 40+/20¢ each. Publications Manager, The Center for Population Options, 1025 Vermont Avenue NW, Suite 210, Washington, DC 20005. 202/347-5700.
With cartoons and simple language, this leaflet helps sexually active teenagers overcome the confusion and embarrassment they may experience when trying to buy and use condoms.

"Crying, Crying, Crying." **"Tossing and Shaking."** 16 other titles. Majority are also available in Spanish. Leaflets. 25-pack, one title, $3.75. R. C. Law & Co., 579 South State College Boulevard, Fullerton, CA 92631. 800/777-5292.
Excellent leaflets. Informative and quick-reading.

Gravelle, Karen, and Leslie Peterson. *Teenage Fathers*. 1992. 202 pp.
Paper, $5.95. Julian Messner, Simon & Schuster Building, Rocke-
feller Center, 1230 Avenue of the Americas, New York, NY 10020.
Thirteen young fathers tell their stories.

Green, Martin I. *A Sigh of Relief: The First-Aid Handbook for
Childhood Emergencies*. 1989. 264 pp. $14.95. Bantam Books, 414
East Golf Road, Des Plaines, IL 60016. 800/223-6834.
*Lots of illustrations and information. Easy to find suggestions for treating
childhood emergencies.*

**"It's About Condoms!" "It's About Sex!" "Play Safe!" "I'll Take
the Condoms!" "In Your Face!" "What's in It for Me?" "I Ain't
Down for Being Called Daddy!"** Four-page phototabloids. Each
title, 50/$17.50; quantity discounts. ETR Associates, P.O. Box 1830,
Santa Cruz, CA 95061-1830. 800/321-4407.
*Highly visual, easy-to-read phototabloids with straightforward information
about urgent health issues. Large photos and simple dialogue depict
realistic situations.*

Klein, Norma. *No More Saturday Nights*. 1989. 272 pp. Paper, $3.95.
Fawcett Books, 38-01 23rd Avenue, Long Island, NY 11105.
*Novel about a teenage father. School librarians tell me the minute this is put
out, teens grab it.*

Leach, Penelope. *Your Baby and Child from Birth to Age Five*.
Revised, 1989. 554 pp. Paper, $19.95. Alfred A. Knopf, 400 Hahn
Road, Westminster, MD 21157. 800/733-3000.
*Beautiful book packed with information, many color photos and sensitive
drawings. Comprehensive, authoritative, readable guide.*

Lindsay, Jeanne Warren. *Do I Have a Daddy? A Story About a Single-
Parent Child*. 1991. 48 pp. Paper, $5.95; hardcover, $12.95. Free
SG. Morning Glory Press, 6595 San Haroldo Way, Buena Park, CA
90620. 714/828-1998. Available in Spanish—*¿Yo tengo papa?*
*A beautiful book for the child who has never met his/her father. A special
sixteen-page section offers suggestions to single mothers.*

_____. *School-Age Parents: The Challenge of Three-Generation
Living*. 1990. 224 pp. Paper, $10.95; hardcover, $17.95. Teacher's
Guide/Study Guide, $2.50 set. Morning Glory Press.
*A much needed book for dealing with the frustrations, problems, and
pleasures of three-generation living.*

_____. *Teenage Couples—Caring, Commitment and Change: How to Build a Relationship that Lasts. Teenage Couples—Coping with Reality: Handling Money, In-laws, Babies and Other Details of Daily Life.* 1995. 192 pp. ea. Paper, $9.95 ea. Hardcover, $15.95 ea. Workbook for each title, $2.50 ea. Teacher's Guide, $15.95. Morning Glory Press.

Relationship series written especially for teenagers. Many quotes from teenage couples already married and/or living together. Also based on nationwide survey of more than 4000 teenagers comparing their attitudes toward and expectations of marriage with the realities of teens already living together.

_____. *Teens Parenting—The Challenge of Toddlers. Teens Parenting—Your Baby's First Year.* 1991. 192 pp. each. Paper, $9.95 each; hardcover, $15.95 each. Workbook, $2.50 each. Morning Glory Press.

How-to-parent books especially for teenage parents. Lots of quotes from teenage parents who share their childrearing experiences. Photos of teenage parents and their children.

_____ and Sally McCullough. *Teens Parenting—Discipline from Birth to Three.* 1991. 192 pp. Paper, $9.95; hardcover, $15.95. Workbook, $2.50. **Video available** to accompany book: **"Discipline from Birth to Three: Guidelines for Avoiding Discipline Problems,"** 54 min., $195. Discounts on sets of four *Teens Parenting* books and on sets of workbooks. Morning Glory Press.

Provides teenage parents with guidelines to help prevent discipline problems with their children and guidelines for dealing with problems when they occur. Excellent supplement for **Teen Dads.**

Marecek, Mary. *Breaking Free from Partner Abuse.* 1993. 96 pp. $7.95. Quantity discount. Morning Glory Press, 6595 San Haroldo Way, Buena Park, CA 90620. 714/828-1998.

Underlying message is that the reader does not deserve to be hit. Simply written. Can help a young woman escape an abusive relationship.

Matiella, Ana Consuelo. *Saturday Night Special: A Story of Choices.* 1989. 27 pp. photonovella. $1.50; 50/$50; 200/$150. ETR Associates, P.O. Box 1830, Santa Cruz, CA 95061-1830. 800/321-4407.

Wonderful booklet. Two couples move from an "I can't talk about it" mindset to being able to discuss their need for mutual protection from AIDS.

MELD Parenting Materials. Nueva Familia: Six books in Spanish and English. *Baby Is Here. Feeding Your Child, 5 months-2 years.*

Healthy Child, Sick Child. Safe Child and Emergencies. Baby Grows. Baby Plays. 1992. $9 each. MELD, 123 North Third Street, Suite 507, Minneapolis, MN 55401. 612/332-7563.
Very easy to read books full of information. Designed especially for Mexican and Mexican American families, but excellent for anyone with limited reading skills. Ask for catalog of other resources for school-age parents.

Parent Express Series: *Parent Express: For You and Your Infant. Spanish edition: Noticlas Para Los Padres. Parent Express: For You and Your Toddler.* Each newsletter, 8 pp. $3.50 each set. ANR Publications, University of California, 6701 San Pablo Avenue, Oakland, CA 94608-1239. 510/642-2431.
Wonderful series of newsletters for parents. Good resource for teen parents. Beautiful photos, easy reading.

Reynolds, Marilyn. *Too Soon for Jeff.* 1994. 124 pp. Paper, $8.95; hardcover, $15.95. Morning Glory Press.
Wonderful novel about a reluctant teenage father. Truly a realistic story about teenage pregnancy from the father's viewpoint.

Robinson, Bryan. *Teenage Fathers.* 1987. 192 pp. $10.95. Macmillan Publishing Company, Inc., Front & Brown Streets, Riverside, NJ 08375. 609/461-6500.
Scholarly research brought alive with frequent vignettes from case studies of young fathers. Debunks the myth of the uncaring teenage father.

Severson, Randolph W. *Dear Birthfather.* 13 pp. $5. Hope Cottage, Financial Office, 4209 McKinney Avenue, Suite 200, Dallas, TX 75205. 214/526-8721.
Good resource for birthfathers. Supportive and informative.

Sherman, Arloc, and Nancy Egg. *The Family Support Act: How Can It Help Teen Parents?* 1991. 35 pp. $4.50. Children's Defense Fund, 25 East Street NW, Washington, DC 20001. 202/628-8787.
Introduction to the Family Support Act of 1988 for teen parent service providers. It targets new education and training efforts for teen parents on welfare. Can help service providers in implementing Family Support Act.

"Talking with Your Partner About Birth Control," "Talking with Your Partner About Safer Sex," "Talking with Your Partner About Using Condoms." Two-fold flyers. 50/$15 per title; quantity discounts. ETR Associates, P.O. Box 1830, Santa Cruz, CA 95061-1830. 800/321-4407.
Easy to read, these leaflets help teens talk with partners about difficult and essential subjects.

Index

MORNING GLORY PRESS
6595 San Haroldo Way, Buena Park, CA 90620
714/828-1998 — FAX 714/828-2049

Please send me the following: Price   Total

Teenage Couples: Expectations and Reality
—   Paper, ISBN 0-930934-98-9   14.95 ————
—   Cloth, ISBN 0-930934-99-7   21.95 ————
Teenage Couples: Caring, Commitment and Change
—   Paper, ISBN 0-930934-93-8   9.95 ————
—   Cloth, ISBN 0-930934-92-x   15.95 ————
Teenage Couples: Coping with Reality
—   Paper, ISBN 0-930934-86-5   9.95 ————
—   Cloth, ISBN 0-930934-87-3   15.95 ————
— *Beyond Dreams*   Paper, ISBN 1-885356-00-5   8.95 ————
—*Too Soon for Jeff*   Paper, ISBN 0-930934-91-1   8.95 ————
—*Detour for Emmy*   Paper, ISBN 0-930934-76-8   8.95 ————
—*Telling*   Paper, ISBN 1-885356-03-x   8.95 ————
—*Teen Dads*   Paper, ISBN 0-930934-78-4   9.95 ————
—*Do I Have a Daddy?* Cloth, ISBN 0-930934-45-8   12.95 ————
—*Did My First Mother Love Me?* ISBN 0-930934-85-7 12.95 ————
—*Breaking Free from Partner Abuse* 0-930934-74-1   7.95 ————
—*Surviving Teen Pregnancy* Paper, 1-885356-06-4   11.95————
School-Age Parents: Three-Generation Living
—   Paper, ISBN 0-930934-36-9   10.95 ————
Teens Parenting—Your Pregnancy and Newborn Journey
—   Paper, ISBN 0-930934-50-4   9.95 ————
—   Cloth, ISBN 0-930934-51-2   15.95 ————
Easier Reading Edition—*Pregnancy and Newborn Journey*
—   Paper, ISBN 0-930934-61-x   9.95 ————
Spanish—Adolescentes como padres—La jornada . . .
—   Paper, ISBN 0-930934-69-5   9.95 ————
Teens Parenting—Your Baby's First Year
—   Paper, ISBN 0-930934-52-0   9.95 ————
Teens Parenting—Challenge of Toddlers
—   Paper, ISBN 0-930934-58-x   9.95————
Teens Parenting—Discipline from Birth to Three
—   Paper, ISBN 0-930934-54-7   9.95————
—**VIDEO: "Discipline from Birth to Three"**   195.00 ————
—**VIDEO: "Your Baby's First Year"**   195.00 ————

                                   TOTAL ————

Please add postage: 10% of total—Min., $3.00
California residents add 7.75% sales tax   ————
                                   TOTAL ————

Ask about quantity discounts, Teacher, Student Guides.
Prepayment requested. School/library purchase orders accepted.
If not satisfied, return in 15 days for refund.

NAME ——————————————————————

ADDRESS ————————————————————
——————————————————————————